A Guide,

TO THE

PEAK OF DERBYSHIRE,

CONTAINING A GONCISE ACCOUNT OF

BUXTON, MATLOCK,

AND

CASTLETON,

AND OTHER REMARKABLE PLACES AND OBJECTS

CHIEFLY IN THE

NORTHERLY PARTS

Of that very Interesting County.

BY THE REV. R. WARD.

THE SEVENTH EDITION.

E. J. MORTEN (Publishers)
Didsbury, Manchester, England.

First Printed 1827
WILLIAM WARD
Constitution Hill,
Birmingham

Reprinted 1972
E. J. MORTEN (Publishers)
Warburton Street,
Didsbury,
Manchester 20

Printed by Scolar Press Limited
Menston, Yorkshire, U.K.

FROM *the rapid sale of several large editions of this Manual, the author of it indulges the hope, that his intention in composing it has been accomplished, and that it has been found useful to strangers who visit the highly interesting scenes in the Peak of Derbyshire. It was far from his purpose to write a* PARTIAL DIRECTORY, *or to swell his pages with* INFLATED DESCHIPTIVE SKETCHES; *but his design was to give plain concise accounts of the various remarkable places and objects, to which he has referred; and having repeatedly visited them, as well as consulted different authors who have written concerning them, he has not hesitated in several instances, as was intimated in former editions, to adopt accounts which had been previously given, when they appeared just and suitable to his purpose. With regard to the present edition he wishes it to be understood, that it has been much enlarged and improved, and extended to a greater number of objects than the former contained; and he trusts it will be found by those persons, for whose use it is calculated, more worthy of their approbation.*

Matlock Bath, 1827.

CONTENTS.

ROAD SKETCH

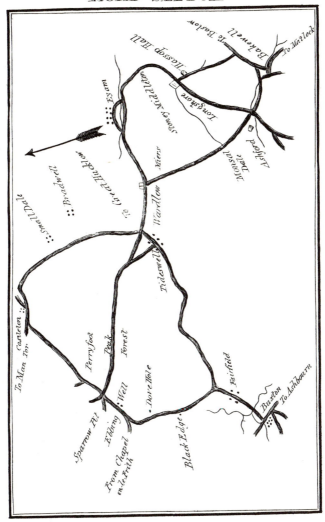

BAKEWELL TO CASTLETON &c.

ROAD SKETCH

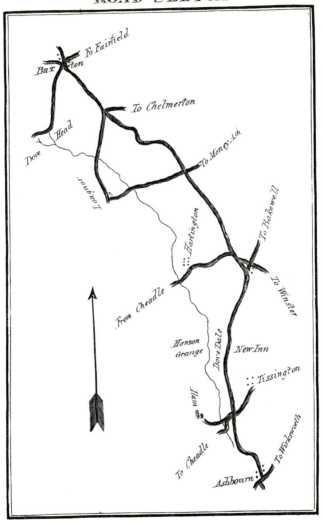

ASHBOURN TO BUXTON.

ROAD SKETCH

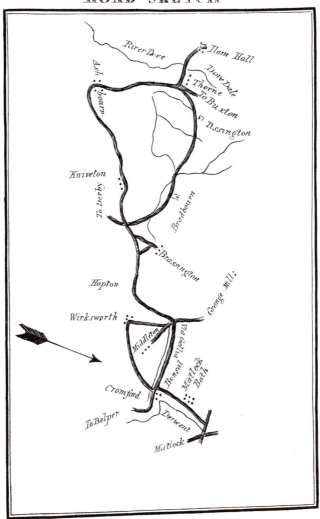

MATLOCK-BATH TO ASHBOURN.

ROAD SKETCH.

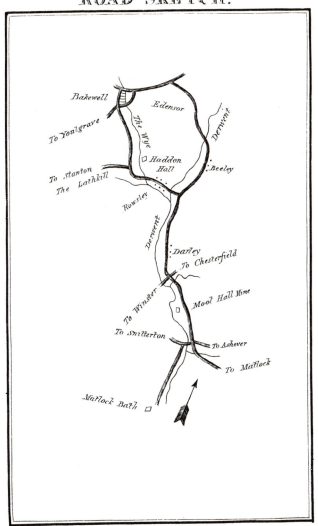

MATLOCK-BATH TO BAKEWELL.

ROAD SKETCH.

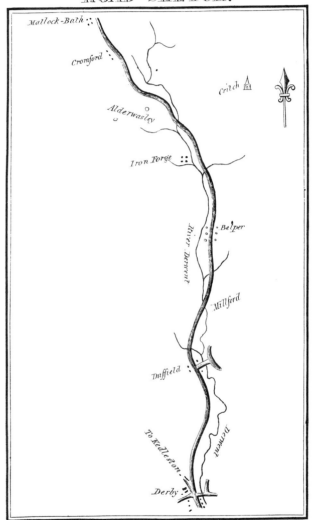

Matlock-Bath

Cromford

Critch

Alderwasley

Iron Forge

River Derwent

Belper

Millford

Duffield

To Kedleston

Derwent

Derby

MATLOCK-BATH TO DERBY.

ROAD SKETCH.

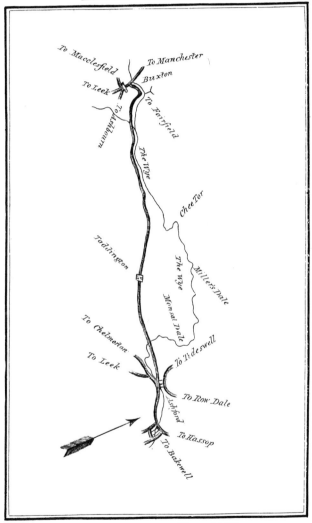

To Macclesfield

To Manchester

To Leek

Buxton

To Fairfield

To Ashbourne

The Wye

Chee Tor

Taddington

The Wye

Miller's Dale

Monsal Dale

To Chelmorton

To Leek

To Tideswell

To Row Dale

Ashford

To Hassop

To Bakewell

BAKEWELL TO BUXTON.

INDEX OF THE DISTANCE

BETWEEN THE PRINCIPAL TOWNS IN THE COUTY OF DERBY.

Distance from Manchester.		Distance from London.
51	Alfreton	142
46	19 Ashbourn	139
82	15 16 Bakewell	152
54	8 14 18 Belper	134
53	11 24 18 16 Bolsover	145
24	25 21 12 30 29 Buxton	159
25	24 26 10 28 26 10 Castleton	162
18	28 26 14 32 29 5 8 Chapel-en-le-Frith	163
48	10 22 12 16 6 24 17 23 Chesterfield	150
59	15 13 25 8 24 33 32 34 24 Derby	126
42	11 11 10 8 17 22 20 24 11 17 Matlock Bath	143
48	13 9 11 6 19 20 21 22 14 14 3 Wirksworth	139

The Names of the respective Towns are on the Top and Side, and the square where both meet gives the distance.

The Peak

OF

DERBYSHIRE.

V ERY remarkable is the county of Derby
for its great variety of surface. If we take a
view of it, beginning at its south and proceeding to its north west extremity, we first behold
a champaign country, then gentle eminences
which, by a gradual transition are succeeded
by hills that increase, as we advance, in height
and extent, and terminate at length in that
mountainous tract called the Low Peak, or
Wapontake, and the High Peak. This very
elevated part of the country has its continuity
broken, and is intersceted, in various places, by
vallies or dales abounding with beautiful scenery; and among the hills that compose the
High Peak the most conspicuous are Ax

B

Edge, about three miles south west of Buxton, Lord's-Seat, near Castleton, and Kinder
Scout, near the north west extremity of the
county. According to the late trigonometrical
survey, the altitude of Holme-moss on Kinder
Scout, is 1859 feet, and that of Ax Edge, and
Lord's Seat, which are of equal height, 1751
feet above the level of the sea. From Kinder
Scout, on account of its great elevation, the
view is said to include Stockport, Manchester,
Bolton, Warrington, Chester, &c. and some
of the mountains of North Wales.

In the Wapontake also there are many considerable eminences, and among these Brassing-
ton Moor, Alport Hill near Wirksworth, and
Crich Cliff may be distinguished, as presenting the most extensive prospects. From the
two former places, in a clear day, the Wrekin
in Shropshire is visible, though fifty miles distant; and from a tower, or prospect house,
erected by the late Francis Hurt, Esq. near
Crich, the view extends, not only over a large
part of Derbyshire, but also into the adjoining
counties, and in a favourable state of the atmosphere, even to Lincoln cathedral.

The Peak of Derbyshire, however, though
generally and justly spoken of as very elevated,

does not possess any eminences that can be ranked among the loftiest mountains of our island; but it is here that a chain of hills commences, which extending even to the borders of Scotland, forms a natural boundary betwixt the east and west sides of the northern part of the kingdom.

Though the air of a country so elevated as the Peak must be cold and piercing; yet the protracted lives of the inhabitants shew, that it is a situation not unfriendly to health: but there is one disorder, the bronchocele, that prevails, chiefly among females, not only in various parts of the Peak, but also in places at a considerable distance from it. This enlargement of the glands of the throat is often termed the Derby neck; though that disease is much more endemic in some other mountainous countries, and especially among the inhabitants of the Alps.

It has often been remarked, that a much larger quantity of rain falls in the immediate neighbourhood of mountains than in the midst of extensive plains. The average annual quantity that fell during the ten years ending with 1812 was, at

Chatsworth.............................27·52 inches,

London...24·31 Inches
Nottingham..............................22·79 ———

Violent storms of rain or hail are not unusual in the Peak; but one that far exceeded
any thing of the kind, which the oldest person
remembered, occured in the southerly part of
it about five o'clock in the afternoon of the
twelfth of May, 1811.   Showers of hailstones
fell congealed together in clusters of large
dimensions, the roofs were stripped off from
buildings, trees were either broken off or torn
up by the roots, and the fences were levelled
in the course of this violent hurricane; yet it
is very remarkable that no one suffered any
personal injury from it.

A singular phenomenon that is sometimes
observed at Matlock and its neighbourhood,
is a lunar rainbow.   There appeared a very
beautiful one betwixt the hours of eight and
nine in the evening of the tenth of September, 1802; and another betwixt seven and
eight in the evening of the first of October,
1803.   In this county also was observed that
extraordinary luminous arch, undoubtedly of
the electric kind, which extended from the
eastern to the western horison, and was seen
throughout the kingdom soon after nine

o'clock in the evening of Sunday, the ele-
venth of September 1814. It continued in
full spledour about half an hour, and then
gradually faded away.

When the general survey of the country
was taken, one of the stations of observation
was fixed at Alport hill, where
the latitude was found to be....53° 3′ 43″
and the longitude......................1 32 22 west.

Alport is about four miles south of Matlock;
and as the longitude at these places is the
same or nearly so, the clocks at both should
be rather more than six minutes later than
those in London.

The Peak of Derbyshire has often supplied
a favourite theme to the tourist, and is visited
by a multitude of strangers on very different
accounts; by the invalid, in hopes of deriving
benefit from its salutary waters; by the admi-
rer of the beauties of nature, to view its delightful dales; by the botanist, to inspect the
numerous indigenous plants with which its
varied surface is clothed; by the mineralogist,
to investigate its minerals and fossils; and by
the geologist, to contemplate its diversified
features, examine its strata, and explore its
caverns and mines.

The antiquary also is here gratified with the sight of various objects peculiarly suited to his taste. Our notice of a few of these may be introduced with observing, that there is one very remarkable monument of antiquity not far from Newhaven, an inn adjoining the road that leads from Ashbourn to Buxton. Betwixt Hurdlow House and Pike Hall appear vestiges of a road that the Romans are supposed to have formed betwixt Buxton and their station at Little Chester, near Derby; and at a short distance from that part of it which lies betwixt two and three miles north east of Newhaven is *Arborlow*, or *Arbelows*, a Druidical area surrounded by a ditch and a high rampart or bank. The form of the area is nearly that of an ellipsis, as it measures 46 yards from east to west, and 52 in a contrary direction; within it are about thirty large stones lying on its border; they are rough and unhewn, and are, for the most part, about five feet long, three broad, and one thick; there are also a few stones near the centre of the area; the width of the surrounding ditch is about six yards; and the height of the bank, which encompasses the ditch, is, on the inside, about five; it is apparently formed of the earth thrown up from the ditch, and measures on the top nearly 270 yards. To the inclosed area there are two entrances, each ten or twelve yards wide, opening to the north and south; and on the east side of the southern entrance is a small low or tumulus, into which an aperture was made some years ago, and the horns of a stag were found in it. There are also many lows or barrows on the neighbouring eminences; and in some of them urns, human bones, and other memorials of remote ages have been discovered.

On the north west side of Peak Forest, about two miles from Chapel-en-le-Frith, there was another Druidical monument, similar in form to that at Arborlow; but it is now very much altered by the operations of agriculture.

The names of many villages and single houses in the Peak were evidently derived from the lows or barrows contiguous to them. These barrows have cavities or dimples in their summits; and that they were places of sepulture has been fully ascertained. In the year 1782 an opening was made by some labouring men into the lower extremity of a large one near Chelmorton. They soon came to a vault

containing the remains of several human bodies lying with their heads towards the centre
of the mount. The bones, says Pilkington,
had never been disturbed, and were apparently united at the different joints, but by
the slightest motion were found to be entirely
loose and unconnected: upon examination they
were discovered to be remarkably strong and
sound; the ribs, in particular, were so little
decayed that they would easily bend without
breaking. Those who saw the bones, thought
they were uncommonly large; and it was imagined that the persons to whom they belonged
must have been, when alive, at least seven
feet high: the teeth were sound and perfect.
From the number of bones and skulls, and the
dimensions of the vault, it was supposed that
it contained about four or five bodies; and
though only one vault was opened, it was presumed that others were carried throughout the
whole circumference of the mount, and that
they might be about twenty in number.

A few miles east of Arborlow, and south of
Bakewell, is Stanton Moor, a rocky, uncultivated waste, on which are numerous remains
of antiquity, as rocking stones, barrows, rock
basins, circles of erect stones, &c. which have

generally been supposed of Druidical origin. A just idea of these can be obtained only from inspection; but though even a minute description cannot be satisfactory, yet there is one object so very remarkable, that it must not be altogether omitted here; and that is an assemblage of gritstone rocks close to the village of Birchover, extending in length between seventy and eighty yards, and rising to the height of forty or fifty. They are distinguished by the name of *Rootor* rocks, an appellation derived from the rocking-stones towards the summit. One of these near the east end is a large block supposed to weigh about fifty tons, which might formerly be easily stirred by the pressure of the hand, but is now immoveable, having been forced from its equilibrium by the mischievous efforts of fourteen young men, who assembled here on Whitsunday, in the year 1799. In another part of this singular mount are seven stones, two or three of them of large size, piled on each other, which may be shaken by the pressure of one hand, and that at several places.

It is to be observed, that the huge masses which form the summit of the Rootor rocks, range from east to west along the middle of the hill, and have had a narrow passage, and two chambers, or caves, cut within them. The largest cave has a remarkable sound, and has thence been named the Echo; its length is sixteen feet, its width twelve, and its height about nine. A hollow in the stone which forms the highest point of these rocks, the late Mr. Rooke supposed to have been a rock-basin; he also mentioned a second rock-basin on the north west side.

If the reader desires to have a particular description of the various remarkable objects to be found near this place, viz. Bradley Rocks, where is a large Rocking-stone, Carcliff Rocks, at the foot of which is a small cave, called the Hermitage, Mock-beggars, Hall, on which stand two erect stones, resembling chimneys, &c. he may be referred to Mr. Rooke's account of them in the different volumes of the Archæologia.

It is well known that the country to which these pages principally relate, abounds with deep cavities in its extensive lime-stone strata; yet neither from these openings, nor from any excavations that have been formed by persons working in the bowels of the earth, has there ever been found any opportunity of examining its contents to a greater depth than about 300 yards below its surface : and hence we perceive how justly it was remarked by a very learned prelate, that the endeavours of man to explore the structure of the earth may be aptly compared to the attempts of a gnat to discover the internal formation of an elephant. Yet ought we not, from the little progress, that our most diligent inquiries enable us to make, to be deterred from the perusal of any page of the book of nature, which according to the observation of another ingenious philosopher, is open to all men, and written in characters equally intelligible to all nations; but, perhaps, in no part of the world more than in Derbyshire; for, as he adds, amidst all the apparent confusion and disorder of the *strata* in that mountainous country, there is, nevertheless one constant invariable order in their arrangement, and of their various productions of animal, vegetable, and mineral substances.

The order of the strata is this :

1. Argillaceous Grit,
2. Silicious Grit,
3. Shale,
4. Lime-stone,
5. Toad-stone,

Then lime-stone and toad-stone alternately; but it is to be remarked, that only three strata of toadstone have been found, and that the lime-stone under the third is the utmost limit to which the researches of the miner have extended.

Between the limestone and toadstone are small beds of clay, from which the warm springs are said to issue.

Argillaceous grit is attended with beds of clay, iron-stone, and coal; the two former containing a great variety of the impressions of vegetables; and wherever these forms occur, they are said to be a certain indication that coal is there to be found.

Silicious grit is composed of granulated quartz, or quartz pebbles; very small topazine and rose coloured quartz, in hexagonal prisms, or with double pyramids detached, are found in a yellowish earth near Buxton, and are called Buxton diamonds; other silicious substances found in various parts of the Peak are excellent free-stone employed for buildings, mill-stone grit serving for mill-stones, and chert, horn-stone, or petrosilex used in the manufacture of earthenware. As silex is the chief ingredient of the oldest and most plentiful of the primitive rocks, and is found in rocks of almost every age and formation, it is esteemed to be the most abundant substance in nature.

Shale or *Schistus*, is of a dark brown, or blackish colour, and appears like indurate clay; no impression of animal or vegetable bodies are found in it: it contains sulphur, and it decomposes in laminæ when exposed to the atmosphere.

Lime-stone seems wholly composed of marine exuviæ, and abounds with a variety of shells, entrochi, coralloids, madrepores, &c. in it are found the principal veins or fissures, which contain galena, sulphuret, and native oxide of zinc, a variety of ochres, fluors, barytes, calcareous crystallizations, pyrites, &c. rotten-stone is sometimes found on its surface, particularly near Wardlow Mire and Ashford; it forms a great variety of marbles, some of a light colour, hard, but incapable of much polish is found near the road called the Via Gellia, leading to Hopton, and thence called Hopton stone; a beautiful mottled grey marble, abounding with entrochi, is obtained at Monyash; at Ashford, Matlock, Monsaldale and other places, is found a fine black marble, that will bear so high a polish, as to reflect objects as strongly as a mirror.

Lime has never yet been found in a pure state, but only in combination with some acid. With *carbonic* acid it forms limestone, marble, chalk, and some other substances ; with *fluoric* acid, it becomes fluate of lime, commonly termed in Derbyshire blue John; with *sulphuric* acid, it constitutes gypsum or alabaster. From the fluate of lime, or fluor spar, the well known vases and chimney ornaments are turned with the lathe ; the beautiful colours generally observable in these vases are obtained by the application of heat. The other valuable mineral called *Alabaster*, is employed by the architect for columns and other ornaments, being much more easily worked than marble; it is also turned by the lathe into cups, basins, vases, and other articles. This substance, which is found in nearly a straight line across the kingdom, appears in three adjoining parishes of this county, viz. Chellaston, Aston, and Elvaston, a few miles south of Derby. It lies about eight yards beneath the surface, and is found, not in regular layers, but in large lumps or blocks imbedded together. The thickness of the beds is from two to four yards. Sulphate of lime, or gypsum, when crystallized, is called *Selenite*; when calcined, it is converted into a fine powder called *Plaster of Paris*; the uses of which, when beaten up with water into a paste, for taking casts of gems, busts, and statues, are well known.

Tufa is the most impure, irregular, and porous of all the varieties of carbonate of lime and is continually deposited by streams impregnated with it. That fine deposition of calcareous matter from such waters upon articles immersed in them, and giving them the appearance of petrifactions, is a kind of tufa. In masses it is generally light and cellular; but it is often found compact enough for building; and at Matlock particularly it is much employed for that purpose.

Toadstone is exceedingly irregular in appearance, thickness, and disposition; not laminated, but consisting of one entire mass, and breaking alike in all directions: it often appears of a dark brown colour with a greenish tinge, and superficially full of holes, which are sometimes filled with calcareous spar; mineral veins in the lime-stone strata above and below it are intersceted by this substance; it admits scarcely any water to filter through it; it is only of partial occurrence, and does not uniformly prevail like the lime-stone strata; nor is it like them equally thick, but varies in this respect from six feet to six hundred, filling up fissures in the lower lime-stone strata; and from the different circumstances attending it the ingenious Mr. Whitehurst inferred it to be as much lava as that which flows from Hecla, Vesuvius, or Ætna.

Barytes, so termed on account of its great weight, but by the miners called *Cawk,* is a mineral that abounds in both copper and lead mines.

It only remains to be observed concerning the strata, that, wherever gritstone occurs, it is incumbent on shale, and shale on lime-stone; that where the former are wanting, the lime-stone strata scarcely ever lie horizontally, but are observed to dip towards those parts of the country where gritstone appears on the surface; and that the degree of their declination is various, being very much influenced by vallies, which sometimes cause them to assume an almost perpendicular direction. In consequence of this arrangement the strata, in many situations, are found at the surface, or nearly so; and the miner is enabled to penetrate them in search of lead ore, and carry on his operations with much greater facility and success.

Here, then, let us pause and reflect, that though the treasures of the earth are buried within it, so that they cannot be discovered and brought forth without the labour of man; yet they are not placed so deep as to render his labour ineffectual. And thus hath God ordained in every other case: nothing, but what is worthless, is to be found by the indolent on the surface of life; every thing valuable must be obtained by labour: all wisdom, all science, all art and experience, are hidden at a proper depth for the exercise of man's faculties; and they, who do not spare their labour, shall not be disappointed in their search.

It is not here intended, nor would it be proper in a work of this kind, to attempt any profound reasoning concerning the nature and disposition of the different strata of the earth ; that would be to invade the province of the geologist : but there is one reflection so very obvious, that it may well be admitted here. Every one must have seen what a multitude of different shells, that is, of marine productions, compose the substance of marble and limestone ; and hence the inference seems

D

irresistible, that these bodies themselves must
have been generated in the same element as
those productions, and that the ground on
which we tread must have been long time
overspread by the waters of the ocean.

But we may advance a step farther and observe, that not only the impressions of various
vegetables, but, also the forms of different
animals, have been found, imbedded in the
earth, and this at a vast distance from the
countries in which they are now produced,
and to which they appear by nature to be
confined. Thus, for instance, at Ashford a
small *alligator* has been found in black marble, and also the tail and back of a *crocodile*
said to be now preserved in a cabinet at
Brussels; and may not these fossil bodies be
regarded " as awful memorials of that universal
deluge, which was ordained as a punishment
for the sins of the primeval race of men?"
But upon this subject let us attend to the
words of a learned and philosophical divine.
He observes, that " the Alps, the Appennines,
the Pyrenees, Libanus, Atlas, and Ararat,
every mountain of every country under heaven
where search has been made, all conspire in
one uniform and universal proof, that the sea

has covered their highest summits. If we examine the earth, we shall find the Moose Deer
natives of America, buried in Ireland; Ele-
phants, natives of Asia and Africa, buried in
the midst of England; Crocodiles, natives
of the Nile, in the heart of Germany; Shell
fish, never known but in the American Seas,
together with skeletons of Whales, in the most
inland regions of England; trees of vast dimensions with their roots and tops, at the
bottom of mines and marls, found in regions
where such trees were never known to grow,
nay, where it is demonstrably impossible they
could grow." The conclusion from these facts
cannot be better expressed than in the words
of another excellent writer. Those fossil
bodies, says he, seemingly so useless, do speak
demonstration to our senses; and are a language which is understood by the most common
capacities, having been appointed by Provi-
dence, as so many standing monuments of the
most remarkable of all transactions; and are,
with regard to the history of Moses, the same
as medals to the Roman history.

That there were lead mines in Derbyshire, at
least as early as the times, when the Romans
were in possession of this country, is evident

from several pigs of lead that have been found
with Roman inscriptions.   One that was discovered on Cromford Moor in the year 1777
bore the following.

IMP. CAES. HADRIANI. AVG. ME I. L VI.

which was thus interpreted by that learned
antiquary, the Rev. Samuel Pegge, the sixth
legion inscribes this in memory of the Emperor
Hadrian.

A nother block was found in the year 1783,
in Matlock Bank, bearing an inscription more
difficult to be ascertained, but Mr. Pegge supposed its meaning to be: *The property of
Lucius Aruconius Vercundus, Lead Merchant
of London.*   A third block was also discovered
at Matlock, more recently, having the following letters inscribed upon it;

TI. CL. TR. LVT. BR. EXARG.

It was conjectured by the Rev. R. Gifford
that these letters stand for the words, Tiberii,
Claudiani, Triumviri, Lutudari, Ex Argentaria.
The weight of this pig was eighty nine pounds,
and of the other found in Matlock Bank,
eighty four pounds.

From the name *Odin,* given to one of the
mines near Castleton, it has been inferred, that
they were also known to the Saxons, and that

in times prior to the introduction of Christianity.

We are informed that in the year 835 Kenewara, Abbess of Repton, granted her estate at *Wircesworth* to Humbert, the Alderman, on condition that he annually gave lead, of the value of three hundred shillings, to archbishop Ceoluoth, for the use of Christ Church, Canterbury. At the time of the Norman survey, the mining for lead was undoubtedly carried on to a considerable extent, as no less than seven mines in this county are mentioned in the Domesday Book.

In very early times, the mines and miners were governed by certain customs and regulations, which in the year 1287 were ascertained by a jury under a commission granted for the purpose. A certain proportion of the ore obtained in the *King's field*, that is in the principle tract of the country containing lead, is due to the crown; and the mineral duties from time immemorial have been let on lease. The present farmer of those in the High Peak is the Duke of Devonshire; and of those in the Wapontake of Wirksworth, Richard Arkwright Esq. They have each a steward and Bar-master in the districts they hold of the

Crown: the steward presides as judge in the Barmote courts, where all disputes respecting the mines are determined by juries. The courts for the Peak are held at Monyash, and for the Wapontake, at Wirksworth, where a handsome Moot Hall has been erected. The principle duty of the bar master is, to put miners in possession of the veins they have discovered, to superintend the measurement of the ore, and receive the dues for the lessee of the crown. In general a thirteenth of the ore is due in the King's field, but the proportion taken is seldom more than a twenty fifth. The dish, trough, or hoppet, by which the ore is measured, contains in the High Peak sixteen pints, in the Wapontake only fourteen. The brazen dish, by which others are regulated is kept at Wirksworth.

In the limestone strata of the Peak, lead ore is found in several forms, but most commonly in that of *galena* or sulphuret of lead; that kind called *slickenside,* having a smooth glossy surface ; is found in the Odin mine. If this singular substance is pierced by the miner's tool or divided by a sharp wedge, it first begins to crackle, in a few minutes after, it rends with considerable violence, exploding with a noise as if blasted with gunpowder; and the incautious miners are sometimes wounded by its fragments. This extraordinary phenomenon occurs in the Haycliff and Ladywash mines at Eyam, as well as the Odin mines. In the first of these a prodigious explosion happened in the year 1738; at which time we are informed by Mr. Whitehurst, the quantity of two hundred barrels, each containing between three and four hundred weight, was blown out at one blast. An occurrence similar to this takes place with unannealed glass; if it be scratched, though it be but by a grain of sand falling upon it, it will seem to consider of it for some time, or even a day, and will then break into a thousand pieces.

Another very important production of the mines is lapis calaminaris or oxide of zinc: this is obtained in considerable quantities in the parish of Bonsall, Wirksworth, Matlock, Youlgrave, Castleton, &c. Petroleum or rock oil, being bitumen in a liquid state, is found in the black marble at Ashford; and elastic bitumen, a substance peculiar to this county, much resembling the caoutchouc, or Indian rubber, occurs in the cavities of the Odin mine. This mine extends far into that mountain,

where alone is found the fluor, usually called
Blue John; a substance, which, on account of
its extraordinary beauty, is wrought into a
great variety of elegant forms, such as urns,
vases, columns, &c. Similar articles are also
made of the different calcareous spars, of gypsum or alabaster, and of marble, and are sold in
numerous shops at Matlock, Buxton, Castleton, and Derby.

For further information on this subject, the
reader may consult " Mawe's Mineralogy of
Derbyshire" his " Catalogue of Minerals," or
other works of a similar description.

Among the remarkable vegetable productions of this county may be mentioned valerian,
elecampane, and camomile. Of the two first
only a small quantity is grown here; but about
eighty acres of land are planted with camomile, young plants being obtained by slipping
them from old ones in the spring; and in
September following the gathering of the
flowers commences, and furnishes employment
for a great number of women and children,
who continue to collect them till the flowering
is stopped by frost. The second year's growth
is more abundant than the first; and the
flowers when collected are dried and sold to be

transmitted to the druggists. They are culti-
vated in the parishes of Ashover, Morton,
Shirland, and North and South Winfield.

Messrs. Lysons, in their account of Derbyshire have given from Pilkington and other
authorities the following list of its indigenous
plants, that are either rare or not of general
occurrence.

Dipsacus pilosus	*Between Derby and Spondon*
Galium montanum	*Middleton-dale*
Polemonium cæruleum	*Matlock and elsewhere*
Alisma ranuncoloides	*Between Derby and Burton*
Epilobium augustifolium	*Matlock and Darley*
Daphne mezerceum	*Matlock and Chee-tor*
Paris quadrifolia	*Pinxton and Newton-wood*
Arbutus uva ursi	*Woodlands*
Saxifraga cæspitosa	*Castleton*
———— hypnoides	*Castleton*
Silene nutans	*Middleton-dale*
Arenaria verna	*Amongst lead mines*
Sedum dasyphyllum	*Pinxton*
Rubus chamæmorus	*Moutains bord. on Cheshire*
Ranunculus lingua	*South Normanton*
Trollius europæus	*Litton-dale*
Ajuga Alpina	*Mount above Castleton*
Galeopsis versicolor	*Between Matlock & Duffield*
Arabis hispida	*Middleton-dale*
Cardamine impatiens	*Matlock*
Iberis nudicaulis	*Middleton-dale*

E

Erysimum cheiranthoides	*Near Ashbourn*
Geranium sanguineum	*Near Buxton*
Lathyrus hirsutus	*South Normanton*
Vicia sylvatica	*Near Matlock Bath*
Lactuca virosa	*Matlock*
Carduss eriophorus	*Matlock*
Gnaphalium dioicum	*Near Hayfield*
Viola lutea	*Dovedale and elsewhere*
Satyrium hircinum	*Crich*
Ophrys cordata	*Moor near Chatsworth*
Osmunda lunaria	*Dethick*
Polypodium calcareum	*Middleton dale*
—————dryopteris }	*Chinley hill*
Pteris crispa ⎰	
Lycopodium alpinum	
—————selagnoides	
——————inundatum	
Cyathea regia	*Lime-stone rocks*

———>|<———

THE FOLLOWING ABOUND NEAR BUXTON AND
ELSEWHERE.

Cistus helianthemus	*Dwarf cistus or sun-flower*
Campanula rotundifolia	*Round leaved bell-flower*
Carduus helenioides	*Downy thistle*
Viola grandiflora	*Yellow rock violet*
Parnassia	*Grass of Parnassus*

To these may be added the heaths, such as
Erica vulgaris and Erica tetralix, which give
a beautiful purple tint to the uncultivated
moors of the peak.

Ornithology. In the month of September 1818, a beautiful falcon, a bird that no person remembered to have seen at Matlock Bath, was shot there; and in January 1822, a fine eagle was shot at Lea-wood near Cromford: the extent of its wings when displayed was seven feet four inches and a half, and it weighed eight pounds and three quarters: it is preserved and is now in the possession of Peter Arkwright Esq. of the Rock House. The king fisher and ring ousel are sometimes found by the Derwent, and in the season for grous shooting, the moors abounding with them attract a number of sportsmen to Buxton, who sometimes meet with that singular bird, the dotterel, when in pursuit of their game.

The account that remains to be given of various objects and places alluded to in the title page, may be preceded by a few remarks, and they can be but few, concerning Derby, the county Town, and Kedleston, the elegant Mansion of Lord Scarsdale situated near it.

DERBY.

DERBY is computed to contain at present about twenty-four thousand inhabitants, every year of late having made large additions to its population. It contains five churches, and another with free sittings is about to be added to the number; that of All Saints, is the great ornament of the town. Its beautiful and much admired gothic tower was erected in the reign of Henry the Eighth and is said to be one hundred and seventy eight feet high; the body of the Church is in the Grecian style; and was built after the designs of Gibbs in the years 1723, 1724, and 1725. In the south part of the chancel is the burial place of the noble family of Cavendish, for whom, there are several monuments. Against the south wall is that of the celebrated Elizabeth, Countess of Shrewsbury,* with her effigies in a recumbent attitude. The epitaph after recording her birth and four marriages, with her issue by her second husband, William Cavendish, adds, "hæc inclitissima Elizabetha Salopiæ comitissa, Ædium de Chatsworth, Hardwick and Oldcotes, magnificentiâ clarissimarum fabricatrix, vitam hanc transitoriam XII die mensis Februarii, anno ab incarn. Domini 1607-8, ac circa annum ætatis suæ 87. finivit." Henry Cavendish, grandson of the third Duke of Devonshire, one of the most eminent chemists and natural philosophers of the age, of whom it has been said by Sir Humphrey Davy, that "since the death of Sir Isaac Newton,

---

* An open rupture took place betwixt this imperious woman and the Earl her husband; and Overton, at that time Bishop of Lichfield and Coventry endeavoured to bring about a reconciliation betwixt them. In a long letter written with this view, he observes, "Some will say in yr. L. behalfe tho' the Countesse is a sharpe and bitter shrewe, and therefore like enough to shorten yr. liefe if shee should kepe yow company: In deede my good Lo. I have heard some say sa; but if shrewdneese or sharpnesse may be a just cause of sep-a-con betweene a man and wiefe, I thinke fewe men would keepe their wives longe; for it is a com-on jeste, yet trewe in some sense, that there is but one shrewe in all the worlde, and ev'y man hathe her, and so ev'y man might be rydd of his wiefe, that wold be rydd of a shrewe. *Lodge's Illustrations*, Vol. III.

England has sustained no scientific loss so great as that of Cavendish," was interred in the family vault, in the month of March, 1810.

The other public buildings here are a County and a Town-hall, a handsome Assembly-room, a Theatre, and a General Infirmary. The building last mentioned was erected a few years ago on a grand scale, and no expense has been spared to render it as commodious as possible; but in the opinion of some persons, it appears a subject of regret, that the plan and expenditure were not regulated with so much attention to economy as to render the establishment less dependent on future contributions. The County Goal, though a substantial building, having been deemed defective in several respects, a new one is now erecting, on a much improved and very extensive plan.

As Derby is situated on the banks of the Derwent, several manufactures that require the aid of water, have been established in its vicinity; such as silk mills, cotton mills, white lead works, iron works, &c. here also is a very lofty tower, erected by Messrs. Cox, for the purpose of making shot.

One of the silk mills, which is the first of the kind ever erected in England, was built by John Lombe, an excellent mechanic, who travelled into Italy, to procure drawings or models of the complicated machines employed in the mills there. Having accomplished his purpose, his design was discovered, and he with difficulty escaped the immediate vengeance of the people, who at that time exclusively enjoyed the advantage of possessing such machinery, Returning to this country he obtained a patent in 1718 for the term of fourteen years, but before the expiration of it he died, and it was strongly suspected, that he fell a victim to the resentment of the Italians, which pursued him to his native land, and effected his destruction by poison.

In this town are the marble works of Mr. Brown, which are of great extent, as marble of various kinds is cut here and polished by means of a steam engine and ingenious machinery: it is then formed into elegant chimney-pieces, monuments, &c. &c. and the proprietor is ever ready to gratify the curiosity of those, who are desirous of viewing the different operations carried on in his works.

Equally attentive is Mr. Bloor to the accommodation of those who visit his china works, which were established here about the year 1750 by the ingenious Mr. Duesbury: they have since been very greatly enlarged and improved, and the porcelain made here is celebrated for the superior excellence of its painting; the gilding and burnishing also are exceedingly rich and beautiful.

In the environs of Derby are many pleasant walks; some of them presenting views of the river and rich meadows, which contribute no less to the amenity of the place than to its prosperity; but it is at a Prospect house erected by the late Samuel Richardson, Esq. on Windmill-hill, that the beauty of this extremely delightful country may be contemplated with the greatest advantage.

KEDLESTON & QUARNDON.

AT the distance of three miles from Derby, the late Lord Scarsdale built a handsome inn, for the reception of those strangers, who might wish to make use of a bath within his park, or to visit his celebrated mansion at *Kedleston.* The water that springs up at the bath, is of the sulphureous kind, similar to that at Harrogate, and is much esteemed for its antiscorbutic qualities. The park is about five miles in circumference; and at the entrance into it there is a grove of venerable oaks, some of them of very uncommon magnitude. The road passes through this grove, and afterwards over an elegant stone bridge of three arches to the house, a superb building, three hundred and sixty feet in extent; consisting of a centre,

and two pavilions connected with the main
building by corridors of the Doric order.
That to the right contains the kitchen and
other offices, that to the left consists of the
private apartments of the family. At the entrance a double flight of steps leads to a noble
Portico, which is formed by six columns of
the Corinthian order, each three feet in diameter and thirty feet in height, proportioned
from those of the Pantheon at Rome, and several of them formed of a single stone. These
support the Tympanum, on which are fixed
three elegant statues, viz. of Venus, Bacchus,
and Ceres, and in niches within the portico are
placed two Muses and a Vestal.

Amidst the uniform elegance and splendour
of this noble house, the hall and the saloon
are entitled to particular notice. The former
is an extremely magnificent room, planned after the ancient Greek model, measuring sixty
seven feet three inches by forty two feet, and
forty feet in height. The ceiling rises to the
top of the house, has three skylights in it, and
is supported by twenty fluted columns of beautifully variegated alabaster, twenty five feet in
height. The saloon is of a circular form,
crowned with a dome, ornamented with rich

stucco-work, finished in octagon compartments with roses : its dimensions are, forty two feet in diameter, twenty four feet to the cornice which is extremely rich, fifty five feet to the top of the cupola, and sixty two to the extremity of the skylight. This room is decorated with a chandelier, branches, and exquisite stucco-work by Rose, and presents such a combination of elegance and splendour as is rarely to be seen.

Almost every room of this noble mansion is enriched with paintings of great excellence ; among which a picture by Claude Lorenze in the drawing room, a landscape by Cuyp, and above all a large piece in the library by Rembrandt, the subject of which is Daniel interpreting Nebuchadnezzar's dream, are usually distinguished as entitled to the highest admiration.

It ought not to be unnoticed, with regard to this house, that in it utility is happily combined with extraordinary magnificence; and that in both these respects the skill and ingenuity of the architect, Adams, have here been signally displayed.

The manor of Kedleston (Cheteleston) was, at the time of taking the domesday survey,

part of the large property of Henry de Ferrars:
it was held under the Ferrars family by that of
Curson or Curzon, as early as the reign of
Henry the first. This ancient family frequently
represented the county in Parliament, Sir
John Curzon was created a baronet in 1641.
Sir Nathaniel Curzon the fifth baronet was, in
1760, created baron Scarsdale of Kedleston,
and was father of Nathaniel Lord Scarsdale,
the present Lord of the manor of Kedleston.

Quarndon. At this village, about a mile
distant from Kedleston Inn, is a chalybeate
spring, to which the company have an opportunity of resorting. The water of this spring
is turned to a very deep purple by an infusion
of galls, and at the bottom of the glass, a dark
green colour is produced. It soon loses its
carbonic acid gas, on being exposed to the atmosphere; and the iron which had been held
in solution by the acid, is then precipitated.

Persons of weak and relaxed habits, when
free from fever, derive much benefit and
increase of strength from this water: there are
comfortable lodgings for their reception in the
village, and this place has moreover the advantage of being situated at an easy distance from
the town of Derby.

MATLOCK BATH.

The turnpike used, from Derby to Matlock, passes the pleasant village of Duffield ; also through Milford and Belper, where are extensive cotton mills and elegant houses belonging to Mess. Strutt.   One of the mills at Belper is worked by a wheel of very uncommon dimensions ; the face it presents to the water being no less than forty feet in breadth.

The road from this place has been formed only a few years, and passes along near the fine river Derwent, through delightful vallies, bounded by undulating hills, clothed with rich woods, which in some parts descending to the road form extensive avenues; while here and there the adjacent meadows, waters, and woods being disclosed to great advantage, the eye is charmed with vistas progressively increasing with beauty and interest; till the climax terminates, as it should do, in the romantic vale of Matlock.

The situation of *Matlock Bath* is in the bosom of a deep valley by the side of the Derwent. This river is formed by the confluence of several small streams, which rising in that wild, unfrequented part of Derbyshire, called the Woodlands, are united near Hathersage. It afterwards visits Chatsworth ; and three miles farther southward is augmented by the river Wye, which rises near Buxton, and having passed by Ashford and Bakewell, falls into this river at Rowsely ; then pursuing its course through the middle of the county, the Derwent passes by Darley, Matlock, Belper, and Duffield, and falls into the Trent, a few miles below Derby. Among the vallies of extraordinary beauty, through which these rivers stray, none is so much celebrated as that in which Matlock Bath is situated. But though Nature has lavished numberless charms on this delightful dale, yet little more than a century has elapsed since it first began to emerge from obscurity ; and that in consequence of a spring of warm water being discovered in it. This happened about the year 1698; and the spring having soon after acquired some reputation on account of its medicinal qualities, a house or two were erected near it for the accommodation of visitors. As the number of these increased, the houses were gradually enlarged and rendered commodious; and Matlock in a few years became the general rendezvous of the neighbouring gentry, who passed much time together here, composing, as it were, but one family, and uniting to form a most agreeable society. The reputation of the place was at length more generally diffused; and it has now become the favourite resort of the gay and the valetudinary; of whom there is frequently a greater influx than it can supply with suitable accommodation; though in consequence of two other warm springs being discovered here at different periods, the buildings have been multiplied to such an extent, that they are now computed to be capable of receiving about five hundred persons in addition to the regular inhabitants. Before the discovery of the springs, no trace of a wheel had ever been seen in the dale, which was covered with wood; but, after that event, a road was formed along the western bank of the river. The valley itself is about two miles in length, and it runs, not without several considerable deviations, in a north and south direction. It terminates, towards the north, near Matlock Bridge ; and at its south end it is separated from the populous village of Cromford by an immense limestone rock called *Scarthin* rock, through one end of which the turnpike road has been formed by blasting the stone with gunpowder. It has often been mentioned as a subject of regret that, in doing this, the rock was not merely perforated, and a rude arch left over the passage; since such a vestibule to this romantic dale would have been extremely appropriate, and have produced a very happy effect.

Upon entering the valley here, the eye is presented with a very striking view. The river Derwent, which flows through it with a southern course, here winds towards the east. Beyond it is seen a lawn; on the further side and on a very elevated part of which stands *Willersley Castle*, the elegant mansion of Richard Arkwright, Esquire, backed by high ground and wood. Immediately on the right hand, at the entrance, besides the vast rock mentioned above, there appears at some dis-

tance, on the nearer bank of the river, a neat
Chapel, erected by Sir Richard Arkwright;
and a little beyond it a stone bridge of three
arches. Behind this, farther to the east, rises
a very elevated woody country; and on the
lower part of it there is a house of white free
stone, built in a very pleasant situation by the
late Peter Nightingale Esq.—On the left of
the same entrance into the dale is a high and
steep hill called *Harpe Edge:* this is the termination of that lofty mountainous country,
which bounds the whole valley of Matlock on
its western side. The hill itself is adorned with
many trees, copses and craggy rocks; and when
viewed from Willersley Castle, together with
the prodigious rock in front, the river winding
along below the lawn, the chapel, bridge, and
spacious meadows beyond them, and also the
distant mountains, in many parts covered with
fine woods, the whole may be truly said to form
a scene both singular in kind, and of incom-
parable beauty.

Upon entering further into the dale, and proceeding along the bank of the river, the first
object that occurs is a Calvinistic Meeting-
house; and a little way beyond it, on an elevated site, stands the neat white stone house of

F

Adam Wolley, Esq. commanding a fine view
of most beautiful scenery. Nearly opposite
this house, and a large cotton mill erected at
a short distance from it, begins on the farther
side of the river, a very striking continuous
range of perpendicular rocks, which rising to
the height of more than two hundred feet, and
stretching half a mile in length, forms the
eastern boundary of that part of the valley
where the Bath houses are situated. The summit of this magnificent rampart is crowned
with wood; and the face of it, which is much
curved and very irregular, is softened and rendered pleasing to the eye by spreading ivy,
bushy yews, elms, and various other trees, which
take root and grow in the crevices, and cover
it so nearly, that large portions of grey rock are
only here and there open to the view. The
ground below the rocks falls, by a steep declivity, covered with wood, to the brink of the
river; a circumstance which adds much to the
beauty of the dale.

The first house of the public kind towards
the south is the *New Bath*, a very commodious
Inn kept by Mr. Saxton, and calculated to receive about fifty persons. From this house and
spacious green in front of it, the view of the op-

posite range of rocks is peculiarly advantageous and pleasing. Contiguous to the house
is an excellent garden, in the midst of which
grows a remarkable fine lime-tree, whose numerous branches spreading around to a very
great extent from its trunk, afford a grateful
shade in summer to the company resorting to
it. Immediately beyond the garden is a very
neat and comfortable lodging-house belonging
to Mr. Richard Walker, and calculated for
the reception of upwards of twenty persons. A
few hundred yards further northwards stands
the other *Principal Hotel,* called the Old
Bath, kept by Mrs. Cumming: this house is of
great extent, affording convenient accommodation to about one hundred persons. Besides a
copious spring and a hot as well as a cold bath,
here is a large assembly room ; and during the
season, which begins in spring and continues
till November, assemblies are held in it, chiefly
on Mondays, Wednesdays and Fridays. A billiard table is kept both here and at the New
Bath. There is likewise in the front of this
house a level green and promenade of considerable extent, commanding a very interesting
view, not only of the opposite rocks, the great
ornament of Matlock, but also of a bold and

high hill, which advancing from the western
mountainous country towards the river, seems
here to shut in the valley.   This hill has been
named the *Heights of Abraham*, on account of
the resemblance it was supposed to bear to the
hill so called near Quebec, rendered memorable by the victory and death of the gallant general Wolfe.   It is covered with a thriving
plantation of firs, larches, and other trees: a-
midst which is formed a walk leading in a serpentine, or rather zigzag direction to its summit.   Towards the upper part of it is an open
alcove, and near this, one of the principal cu-
riosities in the neighbourhood, the *Rutland
Cavern*.   From the terrace at the mouth of
this cavern, and other elevated parts of the hill,
there is an extensive and most captivating view,
not only of the Matlock dale and its delightful
scenery, but also of the neigbouring country.
The view is almost equally striking towards
the lower part of the hill, at a house called
the *Tower*, and likewise at another house recently erected by Mr. Rawlinson, an excellent
portrait painter, one of Romney's pupils, whose
merit as an artist has scarcely yet been duly ap-
preciated by the public.   A little way below
the latter is another pleasant house, called the

Villa ; and much upon the same level, but nearer the Old Bath, stands the *Temple,* a very excellent lodging-house, kept by Mrs. Evans, its proprietor, in an agreeable and retired situation. Below this, and nearer the river, are several excellent lodging-houses, and particularly in that very long and handsome building, formerly kept as an hotel. One end of this building is still appropriated to the same use; it is a commodious house, with good stables belonging to it ; it has also the advantage of being near the same excellent bath, which belonged to the large Hotel. In another part of the same building is Mr Mawe's *Museum* or *Derbyshire Ornamental Repository,* containing elegant Vases, Chimney Pieces, and a great variety of other articles formed of marble, spar and alabaster, and also a very interesting collection of Shells, Fossils &c. Admittance into the room is free from expense, and few persons visit Matlock, who do not avail themselves of the indulgence. The proprietor of the Museum, has also opened another Repository at the South end of the same extensive building. That there are several shops here containing beautiful articles, similar in kind to some of those enumerated above, has been already mentioned.   From the Hotel, the adjoining houses, and the opposite green, the views of the river and rocks are peculiarly advantageous: and these views are generally selected by artists who employ their pencils at Matlock.

At the distance of half a mile from the Hotel is the *High Tor,* a rock which, on account of superior magnitude, is far more striking, than any other in the dale The lofty summit of this celebrated rock may be seen from the front of the Old Bath, appearing over the lower parts of the Heights of Abraham.   It stands on the east side of the river ; and is in fact, only the most prominent part of a long range of rocks, similar to that which is opposite the Baths.   The lower part of it is a very high and steep acclivity, covered, in a great measure, with low tangled wood : the upper part is a broad, rugged, and somewhat circular mass of lime and toad-stone, rising perpendicularly to the height of about three hundred feet above the surface of the water.   Beneath it the river rolls over an irregular, stony bed, with a violent and noisy current ; a circumstance that renders more impressive an object that cannot be contemplated without astonishment and awe.   Such must be its effect upon a susceptible mind at all times; but when, in a bright still evening, the beams of the moon, " riding in her majesty," are reflected to the eye from the rippling surface of the river below: and the spacious front of the lofty Tor, and the neighbouring rocks and hills being partially irradiated, exhibit large intermingled masses of light and shade ; no language can adequately express the grandeur of such a scene and the powerful sensations it is calculated to excite.

Concerning this Tor, it may be farther observed, that though it appears so *high*, when viewed from the road in the dale, yet it rises only to a level with the ground behind it ; its summit is therefore easy of access; but scarcely any person can approach the border of it and thence look down to the road and river beneath, without being reminded, " how fearful and dizzy 'tis to cast one's eyes so low!" and without being seized with appalling apprehensions.

The more distant view from this Tor, on account of the winding of the Dale, is much less interesting, than that which is presented from the rocks opposite the Bath houses ; and to the top of these rocks the ascent is rendered

easy by several winding paths formed amidst
the trees that grow upon the acclivity at their
base. One of these passes by an *alcove,* and
is thence carried upwards to the *bird-cage*
situated towards the summit of the rocks.
But in order to arrive at these walks it is
necessary to cross the water, and boats are
kept for the purpose on that part of the river
which is opposite the Old Bath.—These boats
belong to Mr. Richard Walker, and are attended with peculiar advantage, as they afford
to the robust the means of agreeable exercise
in short aquatic excursions; to the languid
and inactive they offer a soothing mitigation
of the sultry heat of summer; and to all persons a pleasing opportunity of contemplating
at successive points of view, the impending
woods and immense range of rock that towers
majestically above them.—On the farther
side of the river the first object presented to
view is Walker's Repository of the various
curious articles made of spar, alabaster, &c.
referred to above: here also is found the
Lovers' Walk, passing along the bank amidst
trees that form a kind of avenue or bower to
its different extremities. At its south end
there is a recess in a rock called *Dido's Cave;*

and here it is divided by a high wall from other extensive walks, that lead to Willersley Castle and the adjoining grounds : these walks by Mr. Arkwright's indulgence, are open to all who choose to visit them, every Monday and Thursday ; and here are to be met with scenes of the most agreeable and impressive kind : but it is at the summit of a projecting rock, above the house, called the *Wild Cat Tor*, that there bursts upon the sight one of the most striking views that the imagination can form, a view calculated to excite both awe and admiration,—the Dale with all its romantic scenery, its rocks and precipices clothed with wood, and the river winding beneath them; here appearing one dark, unruffled expanse, and there rushing down a weir, and amidst large stones in a broad impetuous cataract. And should the spectator, looking down from this lofty station, behold the whole bosom of the dale animated with numerous parties of gay visitants ; some wandering as fancy leads, through the shady walks ; others gliding along on the surface of the water ; all *curis expeditis*, in full enjoyment of the surrounding beauties of Nature, and exhilirated by the strains of musical instru-

G

ments proceeding from the recesses of the
groves; this, surely, must appear to be a scene
truly magical, to which should any one think
of doing justice, his pen or pencil would
attempt it in vain.

The house at Willersley is not shewn, as its
furniture has not been selected with a view to
splendour of appearance, but rather for the
purpose of utility, which this mansion possesses
in an eminent degree. Those expressive words
of the poet, " simplex munditiis," are very
applicable here; the house being no less remarkable for elegance and simplicity within,
than it is for just proportion and symmetry in
its external appearance. It contains numerous
portraits and other pieces by Wright and Bar-
ber; particularly a view of Ullswater Lake by
the former, which was purchased for three hundred guineas; it was the last performance of
that excellent artist, and most highly esteemed
as a *chef d'œuvre* of its kind. The spot where
the house is erected, was previously occupied
by a rock, the removal of which cost Sir R.
Arkwright about three thousand pounds. The
architect was Mr. William Thomas of London.
After the edifice was completed, but before
it was inhabited, it was set on fire by the

heat of a stove, some timber having been incautiously inserted too near a flue, and all that was combustible in it, was consumed. This accident happened on the eighth of August 1791.

On an eminence, near the end of the Cromford canal stands the *Rock House*, inhabited by Peter Arkwright Esq. In this House on the third of August, 1792, expired Sir Richard Arkwright: of the extraordinary importance of whose ingenious inventions the reader can scarcely need to be reminded. His uncommon abilities were evinced, not by those inventions alone, but likewise by the judicious methods he adopted to carry them fully into effect, and to secure to himself a just proportion of the advantages resulting from them. " Multa tuli fecique," were the words chosen for his motto; to a person of his aspiring mind, " Aut Cæsar aut nihil," would have been equally suitable.

The first Cotton-mill that was worked by water, was erected at Cromford; and the place was chosen by Sir R. Arkwright, with his usual sagacity, as well on other accounts, as beause the water there issuing from a sough that has been formed to drain the lead mines,

is always warm; so that no obstruction is ever
occasioned by frost; and the quantity of water
supplied from this source, is subject to little
or no variation. Many persons who visit Matlock, would undoubtedly be much gratified,
if permission were given to inspect the mills:
but as, in such a situation, a general permission would be attended with much incon-
venience, and a partial one would be offensive
to those who did not obtain it, it has therefore
been determined that no application for leave
shall be complied with. Dr. Darwin's description of these works shews that true genius
can adorn any subject however unsusceptible
it may appear, with the graces of poetry;
and his lines will doubtless be perused with
pleasure by any one who has some idea of
the nature of these works, and has not had
that gratification already.

So now where Derwent guides his Dusky flood,
Through vaulted mountains and a night of wood
The nymph, Gossypia, treads the velvet sod,
And warms with rosy smiles the watr'y god;
His ponderous oars to slender spindles turns,
And pours o'er massy wheels his foaming urns;
With playful charms her hoary lover wins,
And wheels his trident—while the Monarch spins.

First with nice eye emerging Naïads cull
From leathery pods the vegetable wool;
With wiry teeth *revolving cards* release
The tangled knots and smooth the ravell'd fleece;
Next moves the *iron hand* with fingers fine,
Combs the wide card and forms th'eternal line;
Slow with soft lips, the *whirling can* acquires
The tender skeins, and wraps in rising spires;
With quicken'd pace *successive rollers* move,
And these retain, and those extend the rove.
Then fly the spoles, the rapid axles glow;
While slowly circumvolves the labouring wheel below.

To the *external* beauties of Matlock are to be added its *subterraneous* attractions, which contribute to excite the admiration of strangers: these consist of several caverns denominated the Rutland, the Cumberland, the Fluor, and the Devonshire, which though similar in some respects yet differ so much in other, as to induce some persons to visit them all.

"Facies non omnibus una.
Nec diversa tamen, qualem decet esse sororum."

The limestone strata in the mountainous parts of Derbyshire, or as they are there termed the measures, lying very irregularly, appear to be so broken and rent assunder that large clefts or caverns are sometimes found in them and laid open by miners, when pursuing their labours. These spacious apertures, when first discovered, generally contain a brilliant display of crystallizations, which fail not to prove attractive to the curious, who wish to penetrate into those secret laboratories of Nature.

> Here ranging through her vaulted ways,
> On Nature's alchymy you gaze,
> See how she forms the gem, the ore,
> And all her Magazines explore.

The Rutland Cavern, in the heights of Abraham is remarkably easy of access: the first part of it is a long level path formed with great labour by miners in the solid limestone, leading to several very lofty cavities and vaults of great extent, ramifying, as it were, and spreading in different directions. At the side of one of these, an easy ascent by a great number of steps, conducts the visitor to numerous other cavities and vaulted passages amidst rocks of the most grotesque forms and craggy appearance, extending far into the inner part of the mountain. This cavern contains some springs of clear water, and is adorned with various brilliant crystallizations, and different metallic ores, which are here commodiously presented to the view in their native state.

The view from the *Heights* of the romantic dale below, which appears very striking at all times, is peculiarly so to the spectator, when having traversed this extensive cavern, he first emerges from the dark recesses of it.

The *Cumberland* is a single cavern formed by the union of two,* which have been visited as objects of curiosity more than thirty years. This is shewn by Mr. Peter Smedly, who keeps a spar shop opposite Walker's lodging house, and is situated at a considerable distance up the hill behind that and the New Bath. It extends to a very great length, and possesses this advantage, that the visitor is not obliged to retrace his steps to the part where he entered, but finds and exit at the other end of it. The roofs of the numerous cavities within it are of a different kind from those in the Rutland cavern, having less the appearance of arches; and a multitude of massy stones lying within them appear to have fallen from the roofs above through some violent concussion of the earth, by which they have been disjoined and thrown into horrid confusion : several parts of this cavern also have a very brilliant appearance; and exhibit different substances that will be

* This cavern is sometimes divided, as it was formerly, into two by the disunion of the proprietors; and consequently the visit thither is not attended with the advantage mentioned above.

inspected by the curious mineralogist with great interest and satisfaction.

The *Fluor cavern* is situated towards the top of the wood behind the Old Bath, and though not so extensive as either of those just mentioned, it will not on that account, by many persons who are inclined to visit the caverns, be thought undeserving of particular notice. The way up the wood has lately been improved, and the trouble of ascending it is compensated by the view of the scenery it exhibits: the passage into the cavern is rendered commodious, and the *souterrain* visit easy and agreeable. The different spars in this, as well as in the other caverns, are very brilliant and interesting; the strangly grotesque forms of the objects it contains highly amusing; and the numerous lights placed in its various recesses produce a very impressive and pleasing effect.

One circumstance which particularly recommends a visit to this cavern, is its proximity to certain rocks, formerly called the *Dungeon Tors*, but recently the Romantic Rocks.

Of these rocks some idea may, perhaps, be formed from the following account. There is a lofty hill or precipice covered with wood, and beneath it a vast mass of limestone, having a perpendicular face, in some parts fifty or sixty feet high. This face may be considered as divided into two portions running in different directions, in such a manner, that they would form nearly a right angle at their junction, were there not in that part a projection of the rock, causing it to form two angles instead of one. From these angles, in one of which is the mouth of a mine, several very large fragments have separated, and what is very remarkable, they remain in an erect posture; some of them rising to a great height, and consisting of several enormous stones piled one upon another in the regular manner of mason-work. The passage betwixt these detached cliffs and the parent rock, if it may be so termed, varies in breadth from four to ten, or twelve feet, and is about thirty yards in length. It is decorated on each side with moss, yew, and pendent ivy; and the gloominess of it is much depened by the numerous trees that grow on the steep high hill above, and hang over it; the whole forming a romantic group not easy to be described. The ground adjoining these rocks is overspread with a multitude of stones of large size, covered with moss and wild plants; and amidst them are numerous tall ashes and elms,

H

some of them invested with a mantle of ivy to
their very summits. In short there is not any
thing near Matlock that more deserves inspection than these very remarkable rocks: how
surprising then is it, that a late *Derbyshire
Tourist* should have represented them as "objects too trifling to claim attention"! His mo-
tive can only be guessed at, if indeed his own
words do not betray it; but the fact is, that
those who are in search of *picturesque* rocky
scenery and delight *themselves with picturesque*
description, may here find much to gratify their
taste, if they really have any; nor are these
rocks less worthy of attention than Chee Tor,
the High Tor, or any other of those Tors, on
the deliniation of which they dwell with so
much apparent satisfaction.

The *Devonshire Cavern*, discovered and
shewn in the year 1823, is situated in the hill
that rises above the public garden called the
Botanic Garden, which is very frequently
visited for the sake of the fruit, and of a great
variety of plants and flowers, with which it
abounds. The garden belongs to E. Bown,
who shews the Cavern, which is said to extend
about three hundred yards into the hill: it has
long winding paths, deep recesses, large ca-

vities, massy pillars, and detached stones within
it; and both in this respect, and in its numerous
sparry decorations and mineral ores, it greatly
resembles the caverns already described. A
circumstance however, in one part of it, which
distinguishes this from others, is an immense
roof of stone, no less than two hundred feet
long, and forty broad, having a face regular
and flat as the ceiling of a room. Another
advantage it also possesses, of which the Cumberland cavern is sometimes deprived by the
discord of its owners; the visitor is conducted
to an exit near its farther extremity, where he
finds himself, perhaps unexpectedly, on a terrace, that commands a most impressive view of
the valley beneath, and of a landscape trans-
cendently beautiful and extensive, similar to
that which is presented at the mouth of the
Rutland cavern.

Another cavern, or as it is called, a *Grotto*,
has been more recently discovered under the
High Tor; at the base of which certain miners,
regardless of the old maxim, "spem pretio
non emo," have been carrying on very expen-
sive operations with a view for searching for
mineral treasures; but so uncertain is the issue
of these pursuits, that their produce may per-

haps, be exceeded even by the petty gains arising from the exhibition of the *High Tor Grotto*, (so it is termed)—which compared with any of the caverns cannot be said to be of great extent, but it is so completely lined with a profusion of dogtooth spar, of stalactites, and stalagmites, that it has a strong claim to public notice.

The Matlock water springing in great abundance from limestone rocks is of the clearest kind, and having a temprature of sixty eight degrees, it has a claim to be admitted into the short list of thermal waters, that are to be found in England. It has not been analysed with much exactness; but it has been found to contain a small quantity of neutral salt, probably muriat of soda, and about as much of earthly salt, which is chiefly calcareous. Its calcareous contents are quickly deposited, when it is exposed to the air, encrusting every substance that is immersed in it. Curious specimens of this incrustation are to be seen at, what are called the *Petrifying Wells* at Matlock ; and of the same nature is the *tophus*, or *tufa*, in the bank on the west side of the river, which is much employed here as a building material.

The great benefit often experienced by in-

valids who visit Matlock, is very strongly
attested by Dr. F. Armstrong in the Medical
Commentaries. He says " I have taken great
pains to examine particularly into the proper-
ties of the Matlock springs, and may with
truth assert that they are of the same nature
with the Bristol water, equal in some cases,
and preferable in many."—After reciting the
unexpected recovery of a young lady, whom
he had lately sent to Matlock in a confirmed
phthisis pulmonalis, he adds, " I have, in the
course of seven years, sent a great number of
patients to Matlock, and in cases where medicine had not the least prospect of being ser-
viceable; all of whom have had perfect and
lasting cures; and may with truth declare, I
have not failed in one instance."—He afterwards observes, "I perfectly agree with Dr.
Perceval, that a larger quantity of Matlock water may be drunk at a time, than any other
mineral water I am acquainted with, owing to
the entire absence of any mineral spirit ; yet it
is always advisable to begin with small quantities. From the want of mineral spirit it is less
apt to throw the circulation of the blood into
irregularities, or quicken the pulse ; and
therefore it must have the preference to Bris-

tol water in phthisis, pulmonalis, hæmoptoe, diabetes, fluor albus &c. In all these I have experienced the most happy effects from it, as well in hysteric and hypocondriac affections, profluvium or deficiency of catemenia, in bilious disorders, in constitutions debilitated by long and severe vernal and autumnal intermittents, in disorders arising from long residence in hot climates, in broken constitutions brought on by hard and habitual drinking, and in weak and depraved appetites."

Dr. Saunders, in his excellent treatise on mineral waters, observes, that Matlock water may be employed in all those cases wherein a pure diluent drink is advisable; but it is principally used as a tepid bath, or at least one which comes to the extreme limits of a cold bath. On this account it produces but little shock on immersion, and is therefore peculiarly fitted for those delicate and languid habits, that cannot exert sufficient reaction to overcome the effects of the ordinary cold bath, and on which the benefits it produces chiefly depend. Matlock water forms a good intermediate bath between Bath or Buxton and the sea, and may be employed in preparing the invalid for the latter.— But concerning the preva-

lent custom of resorting annually to the sea
coast for the purpose of bathing, the author
here cited gives this important caution. " If
we consider, says he, the great difference that
always exists between the summer atmosphere
and the heat of the sea; the bleak exposed
aspect of many even of our most favourite
watering-places, and the keen winds, to which
the bather must often be exposed ; I cannot
but think, that there is a great number of invalids, of young children, and delicate females,
who have been often materially injured in
their health by an indiscriminate use of this
powerful application of cold ; and are thereby
disappointed of the advantages of a more genial climate, and of country air, exercise and
amusement, which altogether form a very
remedial process, and give the great charm to
a summer excursion. But it is not merely in
the warmer months, that Matlock may be
visited by the invalid with the prospects of advantage, he would very probably find it equally
favourable to him in winter; since, to the opportunity of using a tepid bath at pleasure,
may be added the benefit of a mild and tempe-
rate air; the place being effectually screened
from cold winds by the nature of its situation.

Letters are received at Matlock from the
south every evening; coaches pass through
the place, and there is an opportunity of get-
ting goods conveyed thence either by land or
the Cromford canal towards every part of the
kingdom.

Among the different plants which usually
attract attention at Matlock, the principle are
those of the orchis kind, of which the following species are found here:

Orchis bifolia, butterfly orchis has a sweet
scent during night,

   Orchis morio, meadow orchis.
   ———mascula, early orchis.
   ———ustulata, dwarf orchis.
   ———latifolia, broad leaved orchis.
   ———maculata, spotted orchis.
   ———conopsea, red-handed orchis.
   Satyrium viride, frog satyrion.
   Ophrys nidus avis, bird's nest orchis.
   ———muscifera, fly orchis.
   ———apifera, bee orchis.

The flower of the bee orchis is so exact an
image of the bee, as to deceive the eye that
views it at a short distance; a circumstance
which has given occasion to the following
lines:

See on that flowret's velvet vest
    How close the busy vagrant lies ?
His thin wrought plume, his downy breast,
    Th' ambrosial gold that swells his thighs.
Perhaps his fragrant load may bind
    His limbs ;—we'll set the captive free,—
I sought the living bee to find,
    And found the image of a bee.

DOVE DALE.

From Matlock an excursion is frequently made to this dale, by way of Ashbourn. In the church at this town are many monuments: one of which, erected in memory of the only daughter of Sir Brooke Boothby, and executed by the chisel of Banks, does very great credit to the abilities of that excellent artist. This lamented child died at the age of five years and eleven months, and very seldom if ever, has one so young had an equal tribute paid to its memory. On the top of the tomb is an exquisite figure of the girl in marble, lying on her side, and around are inscriptions in English, Latin, Italian, and French: the first of these is in the following words:

" To PENELOPE,
only Child of

SIR BROOKE AND DAME SUSANNAH BOOTHBY,

Born, April 11, 1785.   Died, March 13, 1791.

She was in form and intellect

most exquisite.

The unfortunate parents ventured their all on this frail bark,

and the wreck was total."

At the distance of near four miles from Ashbourn, and one from the Buxton road, is the justly celebrated *Dove Dale.* A very high conical hill in its neighbourhood is called Thorp cloud, near which is the entrance into a deep hollow called Bunster dale. A road through this ravine, after descending about half a mile, leads by a sudden turn into the southern extremity of Dove Dale, a most romantic rocky chasm, through which the river Dove pursues its winding course, dashing over the rude masses that have fallen from the adjoining cliffs. The river in some parts nearly fills the bosom of the dale; and the passenger, unless he steps with caution along the narrow broken path on its bank, is in danger of falling from the slippery stones into the stream. In pursuing this path the eye is presented with numerous rugged rocks of the most grotesque

i 2

forms. In some places they shoot up in detached masses, resembling spires or pyramids, to the height of thirty or forty yards, and are finely ornamented with mantling ivy; in other parts the impending rocks seem to forbid all further progress: some are firm and solid throughout; others are split and dislocated, and appear ready to be overwhelmed by the first tempest that sweeps the dale. About a mile from the entrance there opens on the right a magnificent arch, about forty feet high, and eighteen wide, extending in front of a high precipice, but so entirely detached from it, as to have the appearance of a prodigious massy wall, formed by human hands. Upon looking up through the arch to the rock behind, the eye distinguishes in it the mouth of a cavern; and a path that passes under the arch leads up to it by a very steep and difficult ascent. This cavern, which is not remarkably spacious, is called *Reynard's Hall*; and another at a little distance below, is termed *Reynard's Kitchen*. The opposite side of the dale is covered with a mass of hanging wood, from the midst of which a large, detached, craggy rock starts out to a great height, and forms a very grand and impressive object,

known by the appellation of Dove Dale
Church.

It was at a precipice near Reynard's Hall,
apparently more than three hundred feet
high, that Mr. Langton, dean of Clogher, met
his fate. This gentleman, together with a
female friend, Miss La Roche, both mounted
on the same horse, rashly attempted to ascend
the precipice ; but after climbing to a considerable height, the poor animal, unequal to
the task imposed on him, fell under his bur-
then, and rolled down the steep.

The dean was precipitated to the bottom,
where he was found so bruised and mangled
by the fall, that he expired in a few days,
and was buried in Ashbourn church ; but the
young lady, who had been stopt in her descent by her hair being entangled in a bush,
slowly recovered ; though when taken up,
she was insensible, and continued so for two
days. The horse more fortunate than its ri-
ders, received very little injury.

At a short distance from Reynard's Hall a
vast rock rises on the right, and another on
the left side of the river ; beyond which the
dale loses its interesting character, and is generally quitted near a considerable cavern,

called the *Fox-holes*. From this point it is usual to pass by a farm house, called Hanson Grange, to the turnpike road between New-haven and Ashbourn. Sometimes the visit to the dale, instead of ending, commences at the Fox-holes.

Concerning Dove dale, the ingenious Mr. Gilpin, in his Northern Tour, observes, that " it is perhaps one of the most pleasing pieces of scenery of the kind to be met with. It has something peculiarly characteristic. Its detached perpendicular rocks stamp it with an image entirely its own, and for that reason it affords greater pleasure. For it is in scenery as in life : we are most struck with the peculiarity of an original character, provided there is nothing offensive in it."

When Dove dale is visited, about two miles are not unusually added to the excursion, making it extend to two other places on the borders of Staffordshire. One of these is *Oak-over*, where may be seen some exquisite performances of the most eminent painters, Raphael, Titian, Rubens, &c.—The other place is *Ilam*, the property of Jesse Watts Russel, Esq. who has erected a noble mansion there. The style of architecture made choice of is

that which prevailed in the reign of Elizabeth, but with a mixture of the gothic in some
of its parts, and particularly in the circular
lantern which crowns the edifice, and forms
an ornament that is strikingly elegant and
beautiful.   The adjoining grounds, though
principally consisting of a meadow of inconsiderable extent bounded by lofty rocks, are
uncommonly pleasing from the contiguity of
a rich hanging wood, and the views they
admit of the surrounding country.   But what
chiefly contributes to render them attractive
is this singular circumstance, that two rivers,
the *Hamps* and the *Manifold,* here re-appear
within fifteen yards of each other, after flowing
in distinct subterraneous channels; the former from the vicinity of Wetton, a distance
of nearly five miles northward; and the latter
from Leek Water Houses, about six miles to
the south-west.   That the streams which rise
here are really the same that are ingulphed
in the fissures of the rocks at the above mentioned places, has been proved by experi-
ments made with floating bodies: and that
their waters do not intermingle during their
underground course, is evident from the difference of temperature, which on trial with

the thermometer, is found to be two degrees.—There is a little grotto in the rocks that hang over the river, in which Congreve, when scarcely nineteen years of age, is said to have written his comedy entitled the Old Bachelor. The circumstance here mentioned respecting the Hamps and Manifold have been thus pourtrayed by Dr. Darwin's muse, with the usual brilliancy of his poetical imagination:

Where *Hamps* and *Manifold*, their cliffs among,
Each in his flinty channel winds along;
With lucid lines the dusky moor divides
Hurrying to intermix their sister tides.
* * * * * * * * * *
Three thousand steps in sparry clefts they stray,
Or seek thro' sullen mines their gloomy way,
On beds of lava sleep in coral cells,
Or sigh oe'r jasper fish and agate shells.
Till where fam'd *Ilam* leads his boiling floods
Thro' flowery meadows and impending woods;
Pleas'd with light spring they leave the dreary night,
And 'mid circumfluent surges rise to light,
Shake their bright locks, the widening vale pursue,
Their sea-green mantles fring'd with pearly dew;
In playful groups by towering *Thorp* they move,
Bound o'er the foaming weirs, and rush into the Dove.

ALTON ABBEY.

Another mansion in Staffordshire, distant about seven miles from Ashbourn, and which, though not within the limits prescribed to these pages, yet on account of its celebrity, may be briefly noticed here, is Alton Abbey, the seat of the Earl of Shrewsbury. That venerable structure stands on an eminence, commanding a view of an extensive valley, which together with the hills that form its confines, abounds with beautiful scenery, both natural and artificial, consisting of plantations, water, rocks, and various ornamental buildings, particularly a very large conservatory, lately erected by his lordship. Indeed so much has been done to heighten the beauties of these grounds, that one of the first impressions in the mind of the spectator will probably be, the vast expense that must have been lavished in the decoration of them.

TISSINGTON.

———————

At *Tissington,* a pleasant village only two
or three miles distant from Dove-dale, is the
seat of Sir Henry Fitzherbert, Bart. whose ancestors have resided here ever since the reign
of Henry V. The inhabitants of this village
enjoy, what very few villages of equal extent
can boast of, five perenial springs of excellent
water. They seem not insensible of this blessing, for every Holy Thursday, they observe a
singular custom, called the *Well-flowering;*
that is, they vie with each other in adorn-
ing their respective wells, in a tasteful manner, with beautiful garlands and gay floral
devices. Several days previous to the exhibition all hands are employed in collecting flowers, and overspreading boards with moist clay,

in which they fix their stems close to each other, so as to cover the clay; and the flowers being of different colours, they form a kind of mosaic work agreeable to their fancy, as well as words and sentences suitable to the occasion. The boards, garlands, &c. being thus prepared, are placed close to the wells, to be gazed upon and admired by a multitude of spectators, who assemble from the neighbourhood; but some, perhaps, may think, they should be as much delighted, if, instead of viewing the flowers thus elaborately arranged, they saw them " glowing in their native bed." A sermon, suitable to the occasion, is this day delivered at the church, and a procession is afterwards formed from it to the several wells, before each of which some part of the usual service, either the epistle, gospel, or psalm, is read, and a hymn sung to the sound of musical instruments: the people then disperse to their respective dwellings, which, as there is but one small public house in the village, are freely open to all, and the day is concluded with the utmost hospitality and festivity.

Several allusions in our poets shew, that Tissington is not the only place in our island where a custom of this kind has been adopted :

it is well known to have prevailed in ancient
times, and is said to be observed in some parts of
the continent even at this day, with sentiments,
we may charitably hope, not unsuitable to the
occasion : but, however this may be, if in our
own case, a view of the rich blessings we enjoy
has a tendency to excite in our hearts sentiments
of gratitude to the " Author and Giver of all
good things," this practice, any more than that
of begging a blessing upon our food, cannot
surely be regarded as irrational and supersti-
tious.

A few miles higher up the Dove than the
Dale which has been found so attractive, and
adjoining to the river, stands Beresford, a
place memorable from having been the residence of Charles Cotton Esq. who in conjunc-
tion with honest old Izaach, (Isaac Walton, of
piscatory renown,) wrote that popular work,
the *Complete Angler, or Contemplative Man's
Recreation.*   As in this work Cotton, who
composed the second part of it, has, in a style
peculiarly amusing, described the nature of
the country in which he resided, and the great
difficulty of travelling there, and has also
given a general account of the Derbyshire
rivers, it is presumed an extract of some length

from chap. II. will not be unacceptable to the reader. It consists of a dialogue betwixt the author, shadowed under the name of Piscator, and a traveller termed Viator, whom he accidently meets with on a journey, and with great politeness invites to his house on the banks of the Dove. After they have taken some refreshment at Ashbourn and quitted that place, Piscator thus addresses his companion :—

" So, Sir, now we have got to the top of the hill out of town, look about you, and tell me how you like the country.

Viat. Bless me, what mountains are here; are we not in Wales?

Pisc. No, but in almost as mountainous a country, and yet these hills, though high, bleak, and craggy, breed and feed good beef and mutton—above ground, and afford good store of lead—within.

Viat. They had need of all those commodities to make amends for the ill landskip ; but I hope our way does not lie over any of these, for I dread a precipice.

Pisc. Believe me, but it does; and down one, especially, that will appear a little terrible to a stranger,—though the way is passible enough, so passible, that we who are natives of these mountains, and acquainted with them, disdain to alight.

Viat. I hope, though, that a foreigner is privileged to use his own discretion; and that I may have the liberty to entrust my neck to my own feet, rather than to those of my horse, for I have no more at home.

Pisc. 'Twere hard else. But, in the mean time, I think 'twere best, while this way is pretty even to mend our pace, that we may be past that hill I speak of; to the end your apprehension may not be doubled for want of light to discern the easiness of the descent.

Viat. I am willing to put foward as fast as my beast will give me leave, though I fear nothing in your company. But what pretty river is this we are going into?

Pisc. Why this, Sir, is called *Bently-brook*, and it is full of very good trout and grayling; but so encumbered with wood in many places, as is troublesome to an angler.

Viat. Here are the prettiest rivers, and the most of them, in this country that ever I saw; do you know how many you have in the country?

Pisc. I know them all; and they were

not hard to reckon, were it worth the trouble;
but the most considerable of them I will presently name you. And to begin where we
now are, for you must know we are on the
very skirts of Derbyshire; we have first the
river *Dove*, that we shall come to by and by,
which divides the two counties of Derby and
Stafford for many miles together,—and it is
so called from the swiftness of its current:
and that swiftness is occasioned by the declivity of its course, and by being so straitened
in that course betwixt the rocks,—by which
(and they are very high ones,) it is hereabout,
for four or five miles, confined into a very narrow stream: a river, that from a contemptible
fountain which I can cover with my hat—by
the confluence of other rivers, rivulets, brooks,
and rills,—is swelled before it falls into *Trent*,
a little below Eggington, to such a breadth
and depth, as to be in most places navigable,
were not the passage frequently interrupted
with fords and weirs; and it has fertile banks
as any in England, none excepted. And this
river, from its head, for a mile or two, is a black
water (as all the rest of the Derbyshire rivers
of note originally are, for they all spring
from the mosses,) but it is in a few miles' travel

so clarified by the addition of several clear and
very great springs, bigger than itself, which
gush out of the limestone rocks, that, before
it comes to my house, which is but six or seven
miles from its source, you will find it one of the
purest crystalline streams you have seen.

* * * * * * * * * *

The next river of note, (for I shall take
them as they lie eastward from us,) is the river
Wye: I say, note, for we have two lesser betwixt us and it, namely, *Lathkin* and *Brad-
ford;* of which *Lathkin* is, by many degrees
the purest and most transparent stream that
I ever yet saw, either at home or abroad; and
it breeds, it is said, the reddest and best trouts
in England: but these are not to be reputed
rivers, being no better than great springs.
The river *Wye,* then, has its source near unto
Buxton, a town some ten miles from hence,
famous for a warm bath, and which you are to
ride through in your way to Manchester; a
black water too at the fountain, but by the
same reason with *Dove,* becomes very soon a
most delicate clear river, and breeds admirable
trout and grayling, reputed by those who, by
living upon its banks are partial to it, the best
of any : and this—running down by Ashford,

Bakewell, and Haddon—at a town a little lower called Rowsley, falls into *Derwent,* and there loses its name. The next in order is *Derwent,* a black water too, and that not only from its fountain, but quite through its progress, not having these crystal springs to wash and cleanse it, which the two forementioned have; but it abounds with trout and grayling, such as they are, towards its source,—and with salmon below. And this river, from the upper and utmost part of this county, where it springs, taking its course by Chatsworth, Darley, Matlock, Derby, Burrow-ash, and Alvaston, falls into *Trent* at a place called Wilne, and there loses its name. The east side of the county of Derby is bounded by little inconsiderable rivers, as Awber, Eroways, and the like, scarce worth naming, but trouty too, and further we are not to enquire. But, Sir, I have carried you, as a man may say, by water, till we are now come to the descent of the formidable hill I told you of, (at the foot of which runs the river *Dove,* which I cannot but love above all the rest,) and therefore prepare yourself to be a little frightened.

Viat. Sir, I see you would fortify me, that I should not shame myself: but I dare follow

K

where you please to lead me, and I see no danger yet, for the descent methinks, is—thus far—green, even, and easy.

Pisc. You will like it worse presently, when you come to the brow of the hill: and now we are there, what think you?

Viat. What do I think? why I think it the strangest place, that ever, sure, men and horses went down; and that, if there be any safety at all, the safest way is to alight.

Pisc. I think so too, for you who are mounted upon a beast not acquainted with these slippery stones: and though I frequently ride down, I will alight too to bear you company, and to lead you the way; and, if you please, my man shall lead your horse.

Viat. Marry, Sir, and thank you too; for I am afraid I shall have enough to do to look to myself, and with my horse in my hand should be in a double fear, both of breaking my neck, and my horse's falling on me; for it is as steep as a penthouse.

Pisc. To look down from hence it appears so, I confess; but the path winds and turns, and will not be found so troublesome.

Viat. Would I were well down, though. Hoist thee! There's one fair 'scape! These

stones are so slippery I cannot stand, yet again!
I think I were best lay my heels in my neck,
and tumble down.

Pisc. If you think your heels would defend
your neck, that is the way to be soon at the
bottom: but give me your hand at this broad
stone, and then the worst is past.

Viat. I thank you, Sir, I am now past it, I
can go myself. What's here? The sign of a
bridge? do you use to travel with wheelbarrows
in this country?

Pisc. Not that I ever saw, Sir; why do you
ask that question?

Viat. Because this bridge certainly was
made for nothing else: why, a mouse can
hardly go over it: 'tis not two fingers broad.

Pisc. You are pleasant, and I am glad to see
you so: but I have rid over the bridge many
a dark night.

Viat. Why according to the French pro-
verb, and 'tis a good one, among a great many
of worse sense and sound that language
abounds in—Ce que Dieu garde, est bien
gardé, " They whom God takes care of, are in
safe protection;" but, let me tell you, I would
not ride over it for a thousand pounds, nor fall
off it for two: and yet I think I dare venture

K 2

on foot,—though if you were not by to laugh
at me, I should do it on all four.

Pisc. Well, Sir, your mirth becomes you,
and I am glad to see you safe over; and now
you are welcome into Staffordshire.

Viat. How, Staffordshire! what do I there,
trow? there is not a word of Staffordshire in
all my direction.

Pisc. You see you are betrayed into it:
but it shall be in order to something that will
make amends, and 'tis but an ill mile or two
out of your way.

Viat. I believe all things, Sir, and doubt
nothing. Is this your beloved river Dove?
'Tis clear and swift indeed; but a very little
one.

Pisc. You see it here at the worst: we
shall anon come to it again, after two miles
riding, and so near as to lie upon the very
banks.

Viat. Would we were there once; but I
hope we have no more of these Alps to pass
over.

Pisc. No, no, Sir, only this ascent before
you, which you see is not very uneasy: and
then you will no more quarrel with your way.

Viat. Well, if ever I come to London—

of which many a man there, if he were in my place, would make a question—I will sit down and write my travels ; and, like Tom Coriate, print them at my own charge.

Mr. Cotton having conducted his guest through these perils to his abode, brings him the next morning to his fishing-house, now in ruins. It was a beautiful little edifice, erected on the bank of the Dove, in a kind of peninsula, for the accommodation of his friend Walton, no less than himself, and having, in the front of it, a stone containing a cipher that incorporated the initials of both their names, and the motto *Piscatoribus sacrum,* over the door.

DETHICK.

This is a very small hamlet in the parish of
Ashover, distant about four miles from Matlock Bath, which in the reign of Henry the
Third, belonged to an ancient family bearing
the name of the place. In the reign of Henry
the Sixth, it passed by an heiress to Thomas
Babington, the sixth in descent from whom,
Anthony Babington was executed, with circumstances of unusual severity, for a plot, in
which he had a principal share, formed with a
design of destroying queen Elizabeth, and libe-
rating Mary Queen of Scots, at the time when
she was confined at Wingfield Manor house.
In this desperate project there were many ac-
complices, who prosecuting it with little caution, did not long escape the observation of

Elizabeth's vigilant ministers. Finding their designs discovered, they fled in disguise, but were soon apprehended, and fourteen of them, Babington being one of the number, were condemned and executed in September, 1586. At Dethick there is a chapel dedicated to St. John; it was founded in 1279 by Geoffry Dethick and Thomas Prior of Felley in Nottinghamshire: in the three farm houses near it several vestiges of antiquity are observable; but from the present remains the extent of the ancient buildings cannot be ascertained. The manor of Dethick and the estate are the property of Thomas Hallowes Esq. of Glapwell.

SOUTH WINGFIELD.

The pile of building at this place now in ruins, is situated seven miles distant from Matlock, near the road that leads from that place to Alfreton and Mansfield. This road is in some parts extremely pleasant, particularly beyond *Holloway,* where it commands a view of a spacious valley, through which the Derwent, attended by the Cromford canal, pursues its course to the south; the adjoining hills are clothed with remarkably fine woods; and in an elevated situation to the west is seen *Alderwasley,* the pleasant mansion of Francis Hurt Esq. On the left hand of the road near Chrich rises a lofty hill, on the summit of which the late Mr. Hurt erected a tower, or prospect house, from which the view extends not only

over a large part of Derbyshire, but also into
the adjoining counties, and in a favourable
state of the atmosphere, it is said, even to
Lincoln cathedral.

The spacious and once stately structure at
South Wingfield, cannot be contemplated in
its present very ruinous condition without a
train of pensive reflections. The building was
begun about the year 1440 by Ralph lord
Cromwell, lord treasurer in the reign of Henry
the sixth; it was probably completed by John
Talbot, the second Earl of Shrewsbury, to
whom the reversion of the manor was sold,
and there is no doubt it was one of the principal seats of his five immediate successors. It
surrounded two square courts, was castellated
and embattled, and had a tower at each angle;
that at the south west rises higher than the
rest, and commands an extensive prospect.
That it has been a very beautiful edifice plainly
appears from the remains of the north side of
the principal court: these consist of a porch
and a bow with three Gothic windows, the
arches of which are slightly pointed. The
porch and bow window are both embattled,
having a fascia of quatre-foils and roses running
immediately beneath the battlements. The

arch of the door-way of the porch is very
slightly pointed, and enriched with quatre-
foils; on the battlements over it is a shield with
the arms of Cromwell. The inner walls are so
much demolished, that it is scarcely possible
to ascertain the exact form and dimensions of
the apartments.   Some of them were very
spacious: the great hall, a noble apartment,
measured seventy two feet by thirty six : it is
entirely open to the weather ; and excepting
only a small part now converted into a farm-
house, the rest of the building is equally exposed, and must have been so for a great
length of time, since there are very large trees,
on which rooks have formed their nests, growing within it.   Beneath the hall is a vault of
equal extent with it, the roof of which is very
curiously arched with stone, and supported
by a double row of massy pillars.

   In the year 1568, Mary Queen of Scots,
" whose misfortunes began in her cradle, and
accompanied her, with little intermission, to
her grave," was placed in the custody of the
Earl of Shrewsbury ; and the year after this,
as Camden informs us, " Leonard Dacres formed a plan to release her from her confinement
at Wingfield.   She continued seventeen years

in the custody of the Earl, who resided during
that period, at Chatsworth, Wingfield, and
Sheffield, but chiefly at the latter place: that
she was never confined in the present mansion
at Hardwick is certain, because it was erected
by the Countess of Shrewsbury at a later
period; but she may perhaps have spent some
little time in the old house, and have made
use of the sumptuous furniture still shewn in
that place. It appears from Sir Ralph Sad-
ler's papers published in 1809, that there were
two hundred and ten gentlemen, yeomen, offi-
cers, and soldiers, employed in the custody of
the Queen of Scots at Wingfield in the month
of November, 1584. She was removed thence
to Tutbury Castle on the 13th of Jan. 1585.

The first damage this edifice sustained, was
during the civil wars, when it appears to have
been garrisoned for the parliament, and was
taken by storm in Nov. 1643, by a party of
royalists under the command of William Cavendish, Marquis of Newcastle. It was re-
taken by Sir John Gell of Hopton, the governor, Colonel Dalby, being killed during the
siege; and was afterwards dismantled by an
order of parliament, dated June the twenty-
third, 1646. Since that time it has been suf-

fered to go to decay, excepting only a small part of it, which long continued the residence of the family of Halton; till in consequence of a partition of the estate in 1774, the manor-house having become the property of the late Immanuel Halton Esq. he contributed to its dilapidation by pulling down a considerable part of it, in order to make use of the materials in erecting a house at the bottom of the opposite hill, to the great regret of the admirers of this once beautiful and interesting Gothic mansion.

CHESTERFIELD.

One mile on the right of the road leading to this town, and about five miles from Matlock Bath, stands *Overton Hall*, a small but pleasant seat, in which the late Sir Joseph Banks, the venerable president of the Royal Society, sometimes resided. Near it are some fir trees of extraordinary dimensions; and on the declivity of an adjoining hill is a rocking-stone, called by the neighbouring people *Robin Hood's Mark*, which measures about twenty feet in circumference; and from its position, appears not only to have been the work of art, but to have been placed with great ingenuity. About two hundred yards to the north of this is a rock of singular shape, called the *Turning*

Stone, in height nine feet, supposed to have been a rock idol.

At a short distance to the south of Overton Hall, stands an old farm house called *Raven Tor* house, and near it is a rock, on which a pair of ravens have every year built a nest, though the eggs have been constantly taken; and what is very singular, this house, which evidently owes its name to the circumstance now mentioned, has for a longer space of time than the oldest person can assign, continued to bear it.

Oakover is in the parish of *Ashover,* fom which place it is divided by a hill, and a very pleasant valley, refreshed by the small river Amber that flows through it. Ashover is a respectable village, and in its church, a venerable structure, is a very ancient font, supposed to be Saxon, in shape partly circular, partly hexagonal; it is surrounded with twenty figures cast in lead in the attitude of devotion. Here also are several monuments and inscriptions, chiefly in memory of the ancient family of Babington. In the church yard, behind the chancel, may be seen the following curious epitaph:

" In memory of Ralph Lowe, of Lea, in the parish of Ashover, who died Feb. 12, 1795, aged 84,

> O reader! if that thou canst read,
> Look down upon this stone;
> Do all we can, death is a man
> That never spareth none."

At *Stainedge*, or *Stone-edge cliff*, about
three miles beyond Ashover, and four from
Chesterfield, Mr. Rooke has noticed several
rock basins, and two seats which he supposed
to have had an augurial purpose. This elevated place commands a full view of a fine
woodland scene extending over that fertile
tract of country called Scarsdale. In the
midst of it is *Chesterfield*, an ancient corporate
town, having a handsome church, remarkable
for the form of its spire, which is two hundred
and thirty feet high, and in its structure so sin-
gularly twisted, that it seems to lean, in whatever direction it is approached. Beyond this
town, in the distant horizon, three remarkable
edifices, namely, Barlborough Hall, Bolsover
Castle, and Hardwick Hall, may be discovered;
the first mentioned nine, the second six, and
the third seven miles from Chesterfield.

BARLBOROUGH HALL,

Is the seat of the Rev. Cornelius Heathcote Reaston, who has assumed the additional name of Rodes; he having succeeded his late highly esteemed uncle, **C. H. Rodes Esq.** whose family is of great antiquity, and has flourished many centuries in the counties of Nottingham, York, and Derby. This venerable edifice, which has, in its principal front projecting bows terminating in octagonal embattled turrets, and large transom windows, was erected by Sir Francis Rodes, one of the justices of the Common Pleas, in the time of Queen Elizabeth; and in this, as well as in Hardwick hall may be seen a specimen of the style and decorations made use of in the mansions that were erected in the latter half of the sixteenth century.

BOLSOVER CASTLE.

At the time of the Domesday Survey the manor of Bolsover (or Belesovre) was held by William Peveril, who probably built a castle there: for it is recorded that the castle and manor of Bolsover, being part of his estate, were forfeited by William Peveril the younger, for poisoning Ralph, earl of Chester, in 1153. This castle was afterwards either held under the Crown by a long succession of governors, or was granted from time to time to different persons; till in the year 1613 Gilbert, earl of Shrewsbury, sold the manor of Bolsover to Sir Charles Cavendish, who, as the old castle was in ruins, immediately began to lay the foundation of the present habitable mansion, Huntingdon Smithson being

L

the architect.   William Cavendish, his eldest
surviving son, became successively earl, marquis, and duke of Newcastle.   By this great
and opulent nobleman King Charles I. was
entertained with great magnificence at Bolsover, when he was on his way to Scotland, in
1633.   The expense of the dinner he gave was
four thousand pounds.   Lord Clarendon repre-
sents it as " such an excess of feasting as had
scarce ever been known in England before,
and would be still thought very prodigious, if
the same noble person had not, within a year or
two afterwards, made the King and Queen a
more stupendous entertainment, which (God
be thanked,) though possibly it might too
much whet the appetite of others to excess, no
man ever after in those days imitated."   The
duchess of Newcastle, in her memoirs of her
noble husband, tells us, " the King liked the
former entertainment so well, that a year after
his return out of Scotland, he was pleased to
send my lord word, that her Majesty the
Queen was resolved to make a progress into
the northern parts, desiring him to prepare
the like entertainment for her Majesty as he
had formerly done for him, which my lord
did, and endeavoured for it with all possible

care and industry, sparing nothing that might
add splendour to that feast, which both their
Majesties were pleased to honour with their
presence. Ben Jonson he employed in fitting
such scenes and speeches as he could best
devise, and sent for all the gentry of the
country to come and wait on their Majesties;
and, in short, did all that ever he could to
render it great and worthy their royal ac-
ceptance. This entertainment he made at
Bolsover, in Derbyshire, some five miles distant from Welbeck, and resigned Welbeck
for their Majesties' lodging. It cost him in
all between fourteen and fifteen thousand
pounds." In consequence of the civil wars this
loyal nobleman, unsuccessful in his zealous
efforts to support the royal cause, retired to
the continent; and at Antwerp, where he
chiefly resided, he published his celebrated
work on horsemanship. After the Restoration
he returned to England, and having a little
recovered from the wreck, which had been
made of his fortune during his absence, he repaired Bolsover castle, which had been seized
by parliament, and suffered great dilapidation;
and there he chiefly resided during the latter
part of his life.

Bolsover castle, at present consists of two detached buildings: one of these, to which the preceding remarks relate, and which may properly be called the castle, is a castellated edifice, with turrets, and a tower of larger dimensions at the north-east corner. Most of the rooms within it are small: the dining room, or, as it is called, the pillar-parlour, about twenty one feet square, has in its centre a circular pillar surrounded by a table. Above stairs is a large room called the star-chamber, about forty-five feet by thirty. At the head of the first staircase, a door admits to a lofty wall, about three yards thick, that incloses a garden; and in this garden there is a very curious fountain, which through neglect has lost its use, and fallen into a ruinous state. It is a deep reservoir, ornamented with satyrs, birds, and the busts of eight Roman emperors placed in so many niches around it. On a pedestal in the centre is a rude figure, representing Venus with wet drapery thrown over her arm, and in the act of stepping out of a bath. A very particular account of the Castle and Fountain by the Rev. S. Pegge and H. Rooke Esq. may be found in the Bibliotheca Topographica, No. 32. The mansion itself, which had previously been long uninhabited, has now been many years occupied by the vicars of Bolsover.

Concerning the magnificent range of building, that extends along the grand terrace, and is now without a roof, there have been different opinions as to the time when, and the person by whom, it was erected. Dr. Pegge and Lord Orford supposed it to have been built soon after the revolution; but Mr. Bray and Messrs. Lysons, with far greater probability, fix its date before that period. The last mentioned authors consider the date of Diepenbeck's view of Bolsover (1652) to be decisive of the point; and they add, "it is equally certain, that it must have been erected before the civil wars, indeed before the royal visit, it being impracticable that the king and queen, with their court, and all the gentry of the country, could have been entertained in the mansion already described: indeed from the slight manner, in which the duchess, in the life of her husband, speaks of the additions made by him to Bolsover castle, we think it a more probable conjecture, that the great range of building, now in ruins, was built as well as the mansion which is now habitable by his father. The duke's addition probably consisted of the spacious riding-house, for the practice of his favourite amusment, the smithy, &c."—" It is certain that the state apartments were not dismantled till after the year 1710, at which time Bassano speaks of them as furnished, and describes the pictures there in the several rooms, which are said to have been removed to Welbeck. Of the extent of this structute some idea may be formed from the dimensions of the gallery, which was two hundred and twenty feet in length, and twenty eight feet wide. The castle, in later times, has descended from the families of Cavendish, of Hollis and Harley, to that of Bentinck, and is now the property of the duke of Portland. It stands on the brow of a steep hill, and overlooks a large extent of country : towards the west it commands a fine view of Sutton park, and of the spacious mansion there, which has been the seat of several distinguished families, and has lately become the property of Richard Arkwright Esq.—in the more distant prospect towards the south, the lofty towers of Hardwick are seen among the woods.

HARDWICK HALL.

This stately mansion was erected in the time of Queen Elizabeth by the celebrated countess of Shrewsbury, from whom it has descended to its present proprietor, his grace the duke of Devonshire. It was finished about the year 1597, and not having since undergone any alteration, it may be regarded as a complete specimen of the style of architecture that then prevailed, and of what was esteemed a suitable residence for a person of the first rank. It is built of stone, and round its top runs a parapet of open work, in which the countess's initials E. S. repeatedly occur. The rooms are very spacious, and numerous large windows admit such a flood of light into them that the whole has been aptly enough compared to an immense lantern. The most remarkable apartments are the state room and the gallery; the former sixty-four feet nine inches by thirty three feet, and twenty six feet four inches high, having at one end of it a canopy of state, and in another part a bed, the hangings of which are very ancient. This room is hung with tapestry, above which are figures rudely executed in plaster. The gallery is about one hundred and seventy feet long, and twenty six wide, extending the whole length of the eastern side of the house, and hung with numerous pictures, chiefly portraits, many of which are interesting: among others are those of Queen Elizabeth, Lady Jane Grey, Sir Thomas More, Cardinal Pole, Bishop Gardiner, the Countess of Shrewsbury, Mary Queen of Scots, Sir William Cavendish, the first earl of Devonshire, Colonel Charles Cavendish, and Thomas Hobbes, aged 89.

At a short distance from this Hall there are considerable remains of another edifice still more ancient; but from the style of its architecture, apparent in its ruins, it is conjectured that it had not been built any great length of time before the former was erected. It is known to have been the residence of the Hard-

wicks in the reign of Henry the seventh : from
both buildings there is a very interesting view
not only of the adjoining park, abounding with
ancient and wide spreading oaks, but also of
the distant country.

Hardwick Hall has derived great interest
from its being supposed, that it was one of the
prisons of Mary queen of Scots, and from the
rich furniture and other articles, which she is
said to have used, being carefully preserved
there. A bed, a set of chairs, and a suit of
hangings are shewn, as having been the work
of the royal prisoner: it is very probable, that
this was indeed the case, and that the furniture
was really used by her ; but it is also probable,
that those articles were brought either from the
mansion now in ruins, where she may perhaps,
have passed some little time, or rather from
Chatsworth, before the old hall at that place
was taken down. That they were not used by
her, where they are now, is clear from this
circumstance, that the present hall was not
finished till ten years after her execution, in
February 1587.

M

CHATSWORTH.

Chatsworth is ten miles distant from Matlock, and the road to it from this place is
remarkably pleasant. It passes through Darley dale, and by the church-yard, in which is
a yew tree that measures thirty-three feet in
girth; and though it has now lost many extremely large branches, it still exhibits in its
trunk an extraordinary instance of luxuriant
vegetation.

It is usual for those, whose curiosity leads
them to visit Chatsworth, to leave their equipage at a handsome inn erected at Edensor
on the border of the park, and to walk thence
to the house. This magnificent seat of the
duke of Devonshire, at the time of the Domesday Survey, was held by William Peverel for

the king. The manor, for several generations, is known to have continued in the family of Leche or Leach, and in or about the year 1550 was sold to the family of Agard, of whom it was purchased by Sir William Cavendish.

The ancestor of the noble family of this name was Robert de Gernon, who came from Normandy with William the Conqueror, and contributed considerably towards the success of the expedition. Geoffry de Gernon, one of his descendants, resided at Moor hall in Derbyshire, in the reign of Edward the First. Roger, his son, married the daughter and heiress of John Potton or Potkins, of *Cavendish*, in Suffolk ; and his children, according to the custom of the age, and in compliment to their mother, assumed the name of Cavendish. Roger Cavendish, the eldest, was appointed Lord Chief Justice in the year 1366 ; but was seized and beheaded by the insurgents of Suffolk, in revenge for the death of Wat Tyler, whom his son was reported to have slain. On this son named John, the honour of knighthood, with an annuity of £40. for himself and his heirs for ever, was bestowed for his activity in suppressing the insurrections that were then prevalent. Thomas Caven-

dish, his great grandson, was Clerk of the
Pipe in the Exchequer in the time of Henry
the Eighth, and had four sons; the second
of whom was Sir William Cavendish who, in
consequence of his marriage with the heiress
of Hardwick about the year 1544, became
possessed of Hardwick and other estates.
Having been an active and useful instrument
in the business of the Reformation, he obtained several grants of manors and lands in
Derbyshire, which had belonged to religious
houses; was raised to the dignity of a privy
counsellor, and appointed by king Henry the
Eighth to the office of Treasurer of the Chamber. In the reign of Edward the Sixth, he
purchased Chatsworth, and began to build
on the site of the old hall a mansion which
was finished by his widow, afterwards the celebrated countess of Shrewsbury. How many
noble descendants sprung from his marriage
with this lady, may be collected from the long
inscription on the splendid mural monument
which she caused to be constructed for herself
in All Saints Church at Derby, which has
been referred to in a preceding page. The
inscription is in Latin, and is to the following
effect:

" 'To the Memory of ELIZABETH, the Daughter of John Hardwike of Hardwike, in the County of Derby, Esq. and at length co-heiress to her brother John. She was married first, to Robert Barley, of Barley, in the said County of Derby, Esq. afterwards to William Cavendish, of Chatsworth, Knight, Treasurer of the Chamber to the Kings Henry the Eighth, and Edward the Sixth, and to Queen Mary, to whom he was also a Privy Counsellor. She then became the wife of Sir William St. Low, Captain of the Guard to Queen Elizabeth. Her last husband was the Most Noble George Earl of Shrewsbury. By Sir William alone she had issue : this was three Sons ; namely, Henry Cavendish, of Tutbury, in the County of Stafford, Esq. who took to wife Grace, the daughter of the said George, Earl of Shrewsbury, but died without legitimate issue ; William created Baron Cavendish of Hardwike, and Earl of Devonshire, by his late Majesty King James ; and Charles Cavendish, of Welbeck, Knight, Father of the Most Honorable William Cavendish, on account of his great merit created Knight of Bath, Baron Ogle by right of his Mother, and Viscount Mansfield ; Earl, Marquis, and Duke of Newcastle upon Tyne ; and Earl Ogle, of Ogle. She had also an equal number of daughters ; namely, Frances, married to Sir Henry Pierpoint ; Elizabeth, to Charles Stuart, Earl of Lenox ; and Mary, to Gilbert, Earl of Shrewsbury. This very celebrated *Elizabeth*, Countess of Shrewsbury, built the Houses of Chatsworth, Hardwike, and Oldcotes, highly distinguished by their magnificence. She finished her transitory life on the 13th day of February, in the year 1607, and about the eighty-seventh year of her age : and expecting a glorious Resurrection, lies interred beneath."

Of this lady the following character is given by Lodge, in his Illustrations of British History. "She was a woman of masculine understanding and conduct, proud, furious, selfish, and unfeeling. She was a builder, a buyer and seller of estates, a money-lender, a farmer, and a merchant of lead, coals and timber. When disengaged from these employments, she intrigued alternately with Elizabeth and Mary, always to the terror and prejudice of her husband. She lived to a great old age, continually flattered, but seldom deceived, and died immensely rich, and without a friend. The earl was withdrawn by death from these complicated plagues, on the 18th of November, 1590.

It was the fourth earl of Devonshire, who was one of the first and most zealous promoters of the Revolution, and who, in 1694, was consequently created Marquis of Hartington and Duke of Devonshire. By this nobleman, towards the end of the seventeenth century, the building at Chatsworth was taken down, to make room for the present magnificent fabric, which was finished about the year 1706, and is in every respect suitable for a subject of the first rank and fortune. It is well known that the unfortunate queen of Scots, while in the custody of the earl of Shrewsbury, was some time at Chatsworth: here she wrote her second letter to Pope Pius, bearing date the thirty-first of October, 1570. The tradition that the apartments occupied by her were preserved, when the house was rebuilt, is unsupported by any evidence; but there is no reason to doubt, that the rooms, which bear the name of the royal prisoner, occupy the same site as those which she inhabited.

The building at Chatsworth is in the form of a square, containing a court, within it, having a fountain with the statue of Orion, seated on a dolphin in its centre, and a colonnade on the north and south sides of it.—The south front of the house is one hundred and ninety feet in length, and is enriched with pilasters of the Ionic order, resting on a rustic base; the west front is one hundred and seventy-two feet in length, enriched in a similar manner; it has also a pediment supported by half columns of the same order. The other two sides, though not equally rich with these, do great credit to the abilities of the architect Talman: but the present noble owner of this superb mansion, (the sixth duke of Devonshire) has been of late adding, at a very great expense, a large wing to the north side of it, intended to contain a magnificent Museum, for which he has been making extensive collections, particularly of sculpture; and, *inter alia*, in January, 1819 by his order the marble statue of Madame Lætitia Buonaparte, the work of the celebrated Canova, was purchased at Paris for thirty-five thousand francs.

Over the colonnade on the north side of the quadrangle is a gallery, nearly one hundred feet in length, the walls of which are covered with a very numerous and interesting assemblage of drawings by the most eminent masters. Another large gallery is now elegantly fitted up as a library, with an extensive and valuable collection of books.

Of the paintings at Chatsworth there are few that possess any great merit; those which chiefly deserve notice are the following; the Incredulity of St Thomas, by Verris, or perhaps, Laguene, in the chapel, a very beautiful room wainscotted with cedar, and richly ornamented with carving, painting, and sculpture; the portrait of the duke of Cumberland, and an exquisite one of the late duchess of Devonshire, with her infant daughter, the present

Lady Morpeth, on her knee, both by Sir Joshua Reynolds; also an admirable whole length picture of the first earl of Devonshire, ascribed to Mytens:—two large pictures by Sir James Thornhill, viz. the Rape of the Sabine women, and his Perseus and Andromeda have been noticed, but with little approbation. The walls and ceilings of this splendid mansion have been decorated by the pencils of Sir James Thornhill, Verrio, and Laguerre. Some of the sculpture here in marble or stone is from the hand of that eminent artist Cibber; by whom the altar in the chapel, adorned with the figures of Faith and Hope, the four marble statues on the bridge, the two Sphinxes on the pedestals in the front of the house, and several richly ornamented door-cases, were executed.—The numerous fine carvings in wood, by which it is distinguished, were said by lord Orford to have been executed by Gibbons: but though some of that admirable artist's carvings may, perhaps, have been sent to Chatsworth, there is no good reason to believe that he was ever employed there. These exquisite performances are now with far greater probability ascribed to Young, but assisted by several others

N

and particularly by a native of Derbyshire,
Mr. Samuel Watson, grandfather of the present Mr. White Watson of Bakewell, who is
said to have attained uncommon excellence
as a sculptor both in stone and wood; and it
is even asserted, that the urns, the medallions,
the coats of arms, the wreaths and the roses
that adorn the four fronts of Chatsworth, the
military trophies in the court, and some of
those exquisite specimens of carving in wood,
which have been attributed solely to Gibbons,
were either wholly, or in part, the workmanship of Watson.

The water-works at Chatsworth, once held
in much higher estimation, than they are at
present, were constructed under the direction
of Mons. Grillet, a French artist; they were
begun in 1690, when the pipe was laid for the
great fountain, which throws up water to the
height of ninety feet, and also for another,
which throws it to the height of sixty. The
work was executed by Mr. Cock, a plumber
from London; who, in 1693, made the artificial tree, from the branches and leaves of
which a shower is produced. When the great
cascade is exhibited, a vast quantity of water
rushes, with great violence, from the domed

roof of a round building at the head of it, and from the mouths of lions, dolphins, sea nymphs, &c. its ornaments; and falling into a basin in front of it, from which also several fountains issue, it is thence discharged over a series of stone steps, down a descent of nearly two hundred yards, and having reached the bottom, it sinks into the ground and disappears. These works are supplied by a reservoir, which is said to cover fourteen acres of ground.

Chatsworth house stands near the foot of a mountain, that rises behind it with a gradual ascent, and is finely clothed with wood. On the highest part of this eminence is the hunting-tower, a building which commands a very extensive view, and is supposed to have been erected as a station, where ladies might partake in the diversion of stag hunting. On the opposite, that is the west side of the house, and at a small distance from it flows the river Derwent, over which is an elegant stone bridge erected by Paine; and to the north of the bridge, near the river, are the remains of a tower, encompassed by a moat, and called the Bower of Mary, queen of Scots, it having been her favourite retreat, while she remained at Chatsworth.

The park is said to be nine miles in circumference: it is beautifully diversified with hill
and dale, in many parts adorned with plantations; and beyond these, towards the north,
the dusky mountains of the Peak rear their
heads with an air of extraordinary grandeur
and sublimity.

We are informed by Dr. Kennet, that Mar-
shal Tallard, who was taken prisoner by the
duke of Marlborough in 1704 and was de-
tained in this country seven years, having been
hospitable entertained by the duke of Devonshire at Chatsworth, parted from his noble
host with this fine compliment, " My lord,
when I come hereafter to compute the time
of my captivity in England, I shall leave out
the days of my enjoyment at Chatsworth."—
On the third of September, 1768, the king of
Denmark, being on a tour to the north of
England, dined at Chatsworth.—The grand
duke Nicholas, now emperor of Russia, was
splendidly entertained there by the present
duke on the 8th and 9th of December, 1816.
On the twenty-fifth of July 1818, the grand
duke Michael and his suite also dined there;
and in imitation of his brother Nicholas, who
had planted a tree on the lawn to the west

of the house, he left in the same place a similar memorial of his visit.

In the annals of Chatsworth, one person occurs, the pseudo-philosophic Thomas Hobbes,
whose writings and character give him a claim
to particular notice. He was born at Malms-
bury, Wilts, in 1588, entered at Magdalen
Hall, Oxford, in 1608 and five years after went
to reside in the family of the earl of Devonshire, as tutor to his son, with whom he made
the tour of Europe. Upon the death of his
pupil, who had succeeded to the earldom, he
was appointed to superintend the education
of the young earl, his son, with whom he
again visited the continent; and he became
acquainted with the most learned men of his
age both at home and abroad. His well
known abilities procured him the distinction
of being appointed mathematical tutor to the
young prince of Wales: but he afterwards
returned to the Devonshire family, with whom
he resided till the time of his death. According to the account left of him, he passed this
part of his life in a singular manner. He left
his bed early; walked with rapidity up some
hill for the benefit of his health; returned
and breakfasted; visited the earl, the coun-

tess, and their children; and about twelve
o'clock ate a little dinner by himself without
ceremony. Soon after dinner he retired to his
study, where ten or twelve pipes filled with
tobacco were laid ready for him, he then fell
to his usual employment of smoking, thinking,
and writing. He was often visited by persons
of distinction, with whom he would freely con-
verse; but he could ill brook contradiction;
and whenever strangers were introduced to
him, they were cautioned not to contradict
the old man, or dispute with him. The works
he published sufficiently evince the great extent of his abilities, and it is to be lamented
that such powers of mind were not directed to
better purposes. One of his objects was to
strike at the root of all religion, both natural
and revealed; and while he represented the
scriptures as derived from mere human authority, he endeavoured to banish the belief of
God's moral government of the world, and to
reduce man to the degraded state of animal
nature, which, views a rival and a foe in every
one he meets, substitutes force and cunning for
benevolence, and the mildest virtues of the
heart. When the pernicious tendency of his
works had excited public indignation, and his

treatise De cive and his Leviathan were cen-
sured, in the House of Commons, as intended
to subvert religion and civil government, he
became extremely alarmed; and then would
he often be declaring to those about him, that
he meant no harm, that he was no obstinate
man, but was ready to make any proper satisfaction. In short, he shewed by his recan-
tation and excessive fears, that nature had not
intended him for a martyr: he was resolved not
to suffer for any cause; and it was a maxim
with him, that bad means might be used to
procure a good end, for, said he, if I were cast
into a deep pit, and the devil should put down
his cloven foot, I would readily lay hold of it
to get out." In spite of his philosophy, it is
said, that he was childishly afraid of appari-
tions, and that, when alone, he was haunted
with the most tormenting reflections, and he
would awake in great terror, if his candle
happened to go out in the night. He could
never endure any discourse concerning death,
and he seemed to cast off all thoughts about it.
When in his last sickness it was intimated to
him, that he might obtain ease but no remedy,
he used this expression, " I shall be glad then
to find a hole to creep out of the world at."

He lived to be upwards of ninety, and has left to posterity a melancholy proof, that men of the most accomplished reason do not always think and act rationally, and that fine talents, if perverted, only serve to render their possessors the more miserable.

HADDON HALL.

Belongs to his grace the duke of Rutland, and stands at a distance of one mile and a half south of Bakewell, on a bold eminence shaded with wood, and on the east side of the river Wye, which here winds through a valley greatly celebrated for the fertility of its soil. This venerable edifice is of the castellated form; and its commanding situation, its magnitude, and lofty turrets of gray stone, surrounded with wood, give it an air of magnificence truly baronial. The principal entrance is at the north-west angle, under a high tower; and the numerous apartments of the mansion surround two quadrangular paved courts: they have been erected at various periods, but no part of them appears to be of later date than the middle of the sixteenth century: they seem to have been principally constructed

o

by Sir Henry and Sir George Vernon; but it
is probable that the chapel and hall were built
by their ancestor Sir Richard Vernon, who
died in the year 1452.   In the windows of the
chapel are considerable remains of stained
glass, and in one of them is the date *Millesimo*
CCCCXXVII.   From one of the pillars between the nave and south aisle, formed in the
massy style, which had fallen into disuse before
the thirteenth century, it has been conjectured
that the present chapel was built on the site of
another attached to a more ancient mansion,
erected probably by the Avenells, (the prede-
cessors of the Vernons,) who possessed the
manor of Haddon soon after the conquest:
there is also a font in the chapel in the same
style.   A Roman altar, about three feet high,
was formerly placed near the entrance into the
chapel; it is said to have been dug up near
Bakewell, and the inscription it bore is nearly
obliterated, but it was given by bishop Gibson
as follows;

DEO
MARTI
BRACIACÆ
OSITTIVS
CÆCILIAN
PRÆFCT
TRO . . . .
VS

The great Hall, which is situated between the two courts, is about thirty-five feet by twenty-eight within the screen, which seperates it from the buttery and other offices. This must have been the public dining-room; and at the upper end of it there is a raised floor, where the table for the Lord of the mansion and his principal guests was spread. There is also a gallery supported by pillars on each side of the hall, and on these the minstrels, like "Timotheus placed on high," exhilirated with their strains, and gave additional zest to the festive board below. From the south-east corner is a passage to the great staircase, at the head of which are four or five large semi-circular steps formed of solid timber, and leading into the *Long Gallery,* which occupies the whole south side of the second court. This gallery is nearly one hundred and ten feet in length and seventeen feet wide: it is uncertain, when it was erected; but the oak wainscotting seems to have been put up by Sir John Manners, who married the heiress of Sir George Vernon, in the time of queen Elizabeth. The floor is of oak planks, which tradition reports to have been cut out of a single tree that grew in the garden; and

the steps leading to it are said to have been
formed out of the root of the same tree. The
wainscotting is enriched with Corinthian pilasters supporting arches, between which are
shields of the arms of Manners empaling
those of Vernon: the frieze is ornamented
with boars' heads (the crest of Vernon,) roses
and thistles. The great bed-chamber appears
to have been fitted up about the same time
as the gallery; it has a deep cornice of plaster, with a frieze ornamented with boars'
heads and peacocks; and over the fire-place is
a rude bas-relief in plaster of Orpheus charming the beasts. The chamber between this
room and the gallery has a similar cornice and
frieze. Excepting the gallery, all the rooms
are dark and uncomfortable, and afford striking proofs how much domestic accomodations have been improved since the days of
our ancestors. The principal apartments were
hung with loose arras, which concealed the
doors; so that the tapestry was to be lifted up
in order to pass in or out; only for conveni-
ence there were large hooks, by means of
which it might occasionally be held back.
The doors, few of which fit close, are of the
rudest workmanship; and wooden bolts, strong

bars, and iron hasps are, in general, their only fastenings. The kitchen presents many curious vestiges of the hospitality, which anciently distinguished the residence of an English baron. It contains two vast fire-places, with irons for a great number of spits, various stoves, double ranges of dressers, an enormous chopping-block, &c. Adjoining the kitchen are several small rooms, which were used for larders and other purposes.

The gloomy apartments and general appearance of this antique edifice are said to have suggested to Mrs. Radcliffe some of the traits she has introduced in the terrific descriptions of castles in the "Mysteries of Udolpho."

In the sixth volume of the Archæologia Mr. King, having given a description of this building, observes, that "nothing can convey a more complete idea of ancient modes of living, than is to be obtained on this spot. Many great dwellings, which formerly helped to present the same ideas, are now quite rased and gone; and others are only heaps of ruins, so far maimed, that it requires much attention to make out or comprehend what they once were, or to understand any thing of their original plan; and it is much to be wished by

every lover of antiquities, that this princely
habitation may never come so far into favour
as to be modernized; lest the traces of ancient
times and manners, which are now so rarely
preserved in this country, any where, should
be utterly lost also here."

Haddon, in the time of Henry the sixth, was
the property of Sir Richard Vernon, who was
speaker of the parliament held at Leicester in
the year 1425, and was afterwards governor at
Calais; in which office he was succeeded by his
son, who was appointed Constable of England
for life, and was the last person that held that
important office. Sir Henry Vernon, his son
and successor, was the governor of prince
Arthur, heir apparent to Henry the seventh;
and he is said to have frequently entertained
the prince at Haddon. Sir George Vernon,
the last male heir of his family, became so distinguished by his hospitality and magnificent
mode of living, that he was locally termed
"King of the Peak." On his death, in the
seventh year of queen Elizabeth, his large
possessions descended to his two daughters,
Margaret and Dorothy. The former married
Sir Thomas Stanley knight, second son of Edward, the third earl of Derby; and the latter

Sir John Manners, knight, second son of Thomas, first earl of Rutland of that name. By
this marriage Haddon, and the other estates
in the county of Derby, that had been held
by the Vernons, became the property of the
noble family last mentioned, and have regularly descended to the present duke of Rutland.

The knightly family of Manners, we are
told, was seated during many generations at
Ettal in Northumberland, and known in border history amongst the stoutest champions on
the English Side. But Ettal, a place of
strength, was more than once laid in ruins,
and the lands devastated and rendered "nothing worth," by incursions of the Scots; and
though successive kings rewarded the services
and compensated the losses of these valiant
knights, by grants of lands and appointments
to honourable offices in the north, it was many
an age before they attained to such a degree
of wealth as enabled them to appear with
distinction amongst the great families of the
kingdom. At length Sir Robert Manners,
high sheriff of Northumberland, having recommended himself to the favour of the king-
making Warwick and of Richard duke of

Gloucester, was fortunate enough by a judicious marriage with the daughter of lord Roos, heiress of the Tiptofts, earls of Worcester, to add the noble castle and fertile vale of Belvoir to the battered towers and wasted fields of his paternal inheritance. A second splendid alliance completed the aggrandizement of the house of Manners. The son of Sir Robert, bearing in right of his mother the title of lord Roos, and knighted by the earl of Surrey for his distinguished bravery in the Scottish wars, was honoured with the hand of Anne, sole heiress of Sir Thomas St. Leger by the duchess dowager of Exeter, a sister of Edward IV. The heir of this marriage, in consideration of his maternal ancestry, was advanced by Henry VIII, to the title of earl of Rutland, never borne but by princes of the blood. It was this nobleman's second son, Sir John Manners, that became possessed of Nether Haddon and large estates in Derbyshire, in consequence of his marriage with the coheiress of Sir George Vernon, who died in 1561. Upon the death of George, the seventh earl of Rutland in 1641, that elder branch of the noble family having become extinct, John Manners of Nether Haddon, grandson of Sir John above mentioned succeeded to the title : and upon his son was conferred the farther dignity of a duke in 1703.

In the time of this first duke of Rutland, seven score servants were maintained at Haddon Hall, and it was kept open in the true style of old English hospitality during twelve days after Christmas. This house continued to be the principal residence of the family till the beginning of the last century, when it was quitted for Belvoir castle on the border of Leicestershire. About the year 1760 it was entirely stripped of its furniture; but the ancient tapestry of the principal bed chamber, ornamented with peacocks and monkeys, and the old state bed with an earl's coronet, have been replaced in it. The building is kept in good repair; and in more recent times it has occasionally been the scene of mirth and revelry. When its present noble owner came of age, he gave a ball here ; and another was given by the inhabitants of Bakewell, soon after the peace was concluded, in the year 1802, when nearly two hundred couple danced in the long gallery.

P

BAKEWELL.

This ancient town is pleasantly situated on the west side of the river Wye. Its name is derived from its Bath-well, and in the Saxon chronicle it is called *Badecanwyllam,* a circumstance which induced Mr. Bray to conjecture, that the bath had been long in use previously to the year 924, at which time Edward the Elder ordered a town to be built in the vicinity and strongly fortified. The church is an ancient structure, situated on an eminence, and built in the form of a cross with an octagonal tower in the centre ; from this rose a lofty spire till lately, when the building appearing insecure, it was found necessary to take it down. The church itself exhibits the architecture of different periods. The

external arch of the west door-way is enriched
with Saxon ornaments; and both this, and
another arch on the south side of the church,
and also the ancient sculptured font within
it, have attracted particular notice. Among
the monuments it contains, is a beautiful little
one in memory of Sir Godfrey Foljambe and
his Lady, who were the founders of a chantry
here in the reign of Edward the third. Beneath an arch in the vestry is the tomb of
Sir Thomas de Wednesley, who was mortally
wounded in the battle of Shrewsbury, under
Henry the fourth: his recumbent figure on
the tomb is dressed in rich armour. In the
middle of the chancel is a small alabaster
tomb for the heir apparent of a Vernon who
died in the reign of Edward the fourth : and
in the part called the *Newark* are several
other curious monuments; that being the ancient cemetery of the illustrious family at
Haddon.—Two stone coffins, measuring six feet
six inches within, one of them containing a
metal goblet, were found close to the south
side of the church in August 1817.

A remarkable stone cross in the church-
yard at Bakewell had its sides covered with
sculptured figures, which are now almost

effaced ; and there is another similar to this, but superior in form and sculpture, in the church-yard at Eyam. Concerning the design of these objects it has been remarked that "the cross was frequently fixed at the entrance of the church, to inspire recollection in the persons who approached, and reverence towards the mysteries in which they were about to be present. On the high road the cross was frequently placed with a view to call the thoughts of the passenger to a sense of religion, and to restrain the predatory incursions of robbers. In the market place it was a signal for upright intention and fair dealing, and was in every place designed as a check upon a worldy spirit."

Among the numerous epitaphs in Bakewell church-yard the following on a child, who died at the age of two years and six months, may be thought not undeserving of a place here :

> Reader! beneath this marble lies
> The sacred dust of innocence;
> Two years he blest his parents' eyes,
> The third an angel took him hence:
> The sparkling eyes, the lisping tongue,
> Complaisance sweet and manners mild,
> And all that pleases in the young,

Were all united in this child.
Wouldst thou his happier state explore?
To thee the bliss is freely given;
Go, gentle reader! sin no more,
And thou shalt see this flower in heaven.

Another epitaph of a very different character occurs on a monument at the west end of
the church, erected for an old man and his
two wives, who there sleep lovingly together,
as we are informed by the following inscription:

"Know posterity, that on the 8th of April, in the year
of grace 1757, the rambling remains of the above said John
Dale were in the 86th year of his pilgrimage laid with his
two wives.

This thing in life might cause some jealously,
Here all three sleep together lovingly,
Here Sarah's chiding John no longer hears,
And old John's rambling Sarah no more fears;
A period's come to all their toilsome lives,
The goodman's quiet—still are both his wives.

At Bakewell the Duke of Rutland has
erected a very commodious inn, with extensive
stables, &c. it is kept by Mr. and Mrs. Greaves;
and the accomodations at the Rutland Arms
are so excellent and so well known, that they
have ensured to this house very liberal support. Near the place where it stands was the
ancient bath which, as well as that at Buxton,

was probably known to the Romans. The temperature of the spring that supplies this bath, is sixty degrees of Fahr. the water has been analyzed by Mr. Charles Sylvester, of Derby, and ten wine quarts of it are found to contain

Grains.

Sulphate of lime............75

Supercarbonate of lime 20

Sulphate of Magnesia....22

Muriate of Magnesia..... 1·6

Supercarbonate of iron 3·1

121·7

A spacious bath was erected over the spring about the year 1697, which has recently been put in complete repair, and two shower baths have been added to it. In the use of this bath the visitors at the inn are supplied with an additional accomodation, and in the walks adjoining it they find a pleasant promenade. Mr. White Watson, who makes collections of minerals, and arranges them for private cabinets, and who has a great variety of fossils and relics of antiquity in his possession, resides at the bath, and superintends it.

During the summer season the inn at Bakewell is often crowded to excess, particularly

by persons fond of angling, who have here an
excellent opportunity of persuing their favourite diversion along the mazy current of
the beautiful river Wye. This river, on account of its excessively sinuous course, is said
to measure nine miles, though the distance by
the road is only three, betwixt Bakewell and
Rowsley: the fall of the river also from the
bridge at the former place to its termination
at the latter has been found to be thirty feet:
as therefore it descends in this part of its course
with an almost perpetual stream, and with
very little wood upon its banks, it is extremely
well adapted to the operations of the angler.
The trout and grayling caught in the Wye,
and more especially those that are taken out
of the small river Lathkil, which falls into
it above Rowsley, are highly esteemed for
their superior excellency.

The parish of Bakewell is of very great
extent; its length being more than twenty
miles, and breadth upwards of eight. It contains nine chapelries, one of which is *Ashford*,
or *Ashford in the water*, situated on the Wye,
nearly two miles from Bakewell. Here Edward Plantagenet of Woodstock, earl of Kent,
and after him, the *Hollands*, earls of Kent,

and more recently the *Nevilles*, earls of Westmoreland, had a residence, of which the only
vestage that remains is a part of the Moat. This
estate was sold by an earl of Westmoreland,
to Sir William Cavendish, the favourite of
Wolsey, and still continues in the Cavendish
family, being now the property of the duke
of Devonshire.

Ashford is celebrated for its black marble,
bearing the highest polish, and not to be
surpassed in beauty; and here has been constructed very ingenious machinery for sawing
and polishing it. These marble works, which
were originally established by Mr. Henry
Watson, of Bakewell, are now conducted by
Mr. Brown, who carries on the business to a
very considerable extent both at Ashford and
Derby.

MONSAL DALE.

Whoever travels from Bakewell towards Tideswell, when he has ascended from Ashford and passed by a small house at the third milestone, will find himself on the brow of a lofty and steep mountain; and casting his eyes to the bottom of it, if he is not utterly destitute of a taste for the beauties of nature, he will be struck with the highest admiration by a complete view, suddenly presented, of the charming Monsall Dale,* stretching to the right and left immediately beneath him. Along this delightful dale the lively river Wye pursues its meandering course; and the verdant meadows, through which it strays,

---

* Mons altus, the lofty mountain.

Q

have their beauties contrasted and heightened
in no common degree by the surrounding
mountains; the steep sides of which in some
parts are clothed with long tangled wood, in
others are covered with a smooth green sward,
or are overspread with a multitude of loose
grey stones, and here and there have a large
craggy rock✻ projecting from them. On the
farther side of the dale, a prominent hill,
which rises from it less precipitously than the
rest, is divided for the most part into inclosures
finely interspersed with trees. On this the
eye dwells with pleasure; but towards some of
the more distant summits, the view appears
to terminate in cheerless sterility. The deep
sequestered dale itself may well remind the
spectator of that, in which the Abyssinian
prince is said to have been secluded from the
rest of the world; or when, in his survey of
the charming landscape beneath him, he sees
a building or two embosomed in wood, together
with a slight rustic bridge thrown over the
stream, he will look upon this as a situation
admirably adapted for the retreat of an ascetic,
who, retiring from the world, its cares and its
tumults, should wish to devote the remainder

✻ The Hyrst rocks are seen at a distance on the left.

of his days to solitary and " heavenly pensive
contemplation :" here may he say,

> Inveni portum: Spes et Fortuna, valete :
> Sat me lusistis, ludite nunc alios.

> Now safe in port, let others Hope pursue,
> And Fortune's lure, I bid them both adieu.

MIDDLETON DALE.

The term *Dale*, in Derbyshire, is applied indiscriminately, either when the hills on the confines are so remote as to leave a large intermediate valley, or when they are nearly contiguous to each other and there is very little interval betwixt them. Of the former kind are the spacious and fertile dales, that take their name from Darley and Castleton: of the latter are Dove Dale, and several other dales in the course of the Dove and the Wye: such also is the long, deep, and narrow dale commencing at *Stony Middleton*. Through this, which might rather be termed a defile, or ravine, the road from Chesterfield to Tideswell and Buxton passes beneath rocks which, on the north side especially, are perpendicular,

and bear a strong resemblance to the round
towers and buttresses of mouldering castles:
they rise to the height of three or four hundred feet, and are every where naked except
at a point near the entrance of Eyam Dale.
In this respect they differ from the rocks
at Matlock, which have many of their craggy
features concealed by a multitude of trees
and shrubs growing beneath and upon them.
Large quantities of stone taken from extensive
quarries here, are burnt into excellent lime,
or carried to the iron furnaces at Chesterfield;
and the impressive appearance of the dale is
often increased in a surprising degree by lurid
volumes of smoke issuing from a smelting
house, and in a dark night especially, by
coruscations of light cast upon the rocks from
the fires of the lime kilns erected within it.
Near the entrance of the dale is pointed out a
frightful precipice, to which is given the name
of the Lover's Leap, with more justice, it
seems, than that title is usually conferred:
since it is the uniform tradition of the inhabitants near it, that not quite a century ago, very
early one summer morning, a young woman,
called Hannah Baddely, unable to endure
the pangs of disappointed love, after gaining

the top of this rock, and divesting herself
of her bonnet, cap, and handkerchief, threw
herself headlong from it, in hopes of putting
an end to her woes and life together; but we
are told, that her garments being caught by
bushes in several stages of her descent, she fell
with very little hurt into a saw-pit, partly filled
with saw-dust, at the bottom of the rock : it
is added, that she long survived this attempt
at suicide, and not many years have yet elapsed
since death effected, in the natural way, that
dissolution which this desperate expedient had
failed to produce.

There is a bath at Middleton, not much
resorted to, that borrows its name from St.
Martin : the heat of its water is sixty three
degrees of Fahrenheit, and in its qualities it
resembles that at Matlock.   From the Roman
stations at Brough and Buxton not being far
distant, as well as from coins of that people
being found in the neighbourhood, it seems no
ill founded conjecture, that the reputation of
this ancient bath originated with the Romans.

EYAM.

From Middleton Dale another road branches
and leads up to Eyam, a village entitled to particular notice on account of its having been
visited by that dreadful disease, the plague,
in 1666, a year that proved so fatal to many
of the inhabitants of London. From that city
it was communicated to Eyam, by means of a
box of materials sent to a tailor who resided
there. His whole family, except one person,
became the first victims, from whom the subtile
infection quickly spread throughout the village, and out of about three hundred and thirty
persons, its population at that time, two hundred and fifty-nine were speedily carried off
by the devouring pestilence. Not a few of
the miserable sufferers were hurried to graves

hastily dug for them in places whither their
friends thought they might convey them with
more safety than to the church-yard; and
one inclosure on an eminence above the village, called *Riley Grave Stones*, is particularly
pointed out as the receptacle of a considerable
number of them.   Great occasions are often
observed to call forth signal virtues, and so it
happened in this devoted place.   The excellent Mr. Mompesson, at that time the rector,
could not be prevailed upon by the pressing
intreaties of his beloved wife to quit his flock
in these hours of danger and dismay; he remained at his post, daily visiting and praying
with the sick, and administering to them the
consolation of religion: but not neglecting
any precaution that prudence suggested, h e
directed his parishioners to meet for the purpose of divine service in a deep dell at a little
distance from the village; and there did this
rival of Marseilles' good bishop address his
afflicted audience from the arch of a perforated
rock, which has hence obtained the name of
Cucklet church; rationally concluding that
their assembling in the church would be likely
to propagate the infection.   In the church-
yard is a monument for his wife, who fell a

victim to the disease, in the twenty seventh year of her age. In consequence of an arrangement suggested by him to the earl of Devonshire, the inhabitants of Eyam, being supplied with necessaries left for their use at certain appointed places, were prevailed upon by his influence to confine themselves within the limits of their village, so that the infection did not spread beyond it, though the distemper remained in it near seven months. On account of his conduct on this affecting occasion the memory of this faithful pastor was long cherished and revered by the inhabitants, not of Eyam alone, but of all the surrounding country.

It was after he had himself suffered one of the most grievous calamities, that "flesh is heir to," the loss of an amiable wife, the mother of his two children; and when all hope or expectation of being long spared himself, seems to have vanished, that he wrote the following truly pathetic and pious letter to his friend and patron, Sir George Saville:

Eyam, Sept. 1, 1666.

Honoured and Dear Sir,

"This is the saddest news that ever my pen could write. The destroying Angel having taken up his quarters within my habitation, my dearest wife is gone to her eternal rest, and is

R

invested with a crown of righteousness, having made a happy
end. Indeed had she loved herself as well as me, she had
fled from the pit of destruction with the sweet babes, and
might have prolonged her days; but she was resolved to die
a martyr to my interest. My drooping spirits are much refreshed with her joys, which I think are unutterable.

" Sir, this paper is to bid you a hearty farewell for ever, and
to bring you my humble thanks for all your noble favours; and
I hope you will believe a dying man, I have as much love as
honour for you, and I will bend my feeble knees to the God
of Heaven, that you, my dear lady, and your children and their
children, may be blessed with external and eternal happiness,
and that the same blessing may fall upon Lady Sunderland,
and her relations.

" Dear Sir, let your dying Chaplain recommend this truth
to you and your family, that no happiness or solid comfort can
be found in this vale of tears, like living a pious life; and pray
ever remember this rule, *Never do any thing upon which you
dare not first ask the blessing of God.*

" Sir, I have made bold in my will with your name for
executor, and I hope that you will not take it ill. I have
joined two others with you, who will take from you the trouble. Your favourable aspect will, I know, be a great comfort
to my distressed orphans. I am not desirous that they should
be great, but good; and my next request is, that they may be
brought up in the fear and admonition of the Lord.

" Sir, I thank God I am contented to shake hands with all
the world; and have many comfortable assurances that God
will accept me on account of his Son. I find the goodness of
God greater than ever I thought or imagined; and I wish
from my soul that it were not so much abused and contemned.

"I desire, Sir, that you will be pleased to make choice of a humble, pious man, to succeed me in my parsonage; and could I see your face before my departure hence, I would inform you in what manner I think he may live comfortable amongst his people, which would be some satisfaction to me before I die.

"Dear Sir, I beg the prayers of all about you that I may not be daunted by the powers of Hell, and that I may have dying graces: with tears I beg, that when you are praying for fatherless orphans, you would remember my two pretty babes.

"Pardon the rude style of this paper, and be pleased to believe that I am,   Dear Sir, &c.

WILLIAM MOMPESSON."

Though, when this letter was written, it appears that not a ray of earthly hope remained to cheer the spirit of this excellent man, yet did he escape the perils that surrounded him; and from his great merit, evinced on this trying occasion, there was scarcely any preferment in the church, to which he might not have aspired. All that he accepted was prebends of York and Southwell, and the rectory of Eakring in Nottinghamshire, where he closed a long and useful life most highly esteemed by all that knew him.

Another rector of Eyam was the celebrated Miss Seward's father, and that lady was a native of the place; concerning whom it is sufficient to say here, that she undoubtedly possessed no mean literary acquirements; but that the productions of her Muse are now little thought of, and that very few of her numerous letters, edited by Sir Walter Scott, are distinguished by that ease and simplicity, which give the principle charm to such compositions.

An antique stone cross, which is said to have been found on a neighbouring hill, but which afterwards had long lain neglected, and lost a part of its shaft, has been erected in the church-yard at Eyam. It is covered with a variety of embossed figures, much more distinct than those on the cross at Bakewell. Crosses of this kind, it is generally supposed were constructed by the Anglo-Saxons, soon after the introduction of christianity amongst them. In this church-yard are also many epitaphs from the pen of a votary of the Muses, the Rev. P. Cunninghame, who was many years curate of the parish: his monumental compositions may be easily distinguished from the rest, which are of the kind so graphically described by the poet:

" Their name, their years, spelt by th'unletter'd Muse,
The place of fame and elegy supply;
And many a holy text around she strews,
That teach the rustic moralist how to die."

One inscription from such a Muse occurs
on an humble grave-stone placed against the
south wall of the church, and is in small
capital letters:

HERE LITH THE BODY OF ANN SELLARS
BURIED BY THIS STONE—WHO
DYED ON JAN. 15TH DAY 1731.
LIKEWISE HERE LISE DEAR ISAAC
SELLARS, MY HUSBAND AND MY RIGHT,
WHO WAS BURIED ON THAT SAME DAY COME
SEVEN YEARS 1738. IN SEVEN YEARS
TIME THERE COMES A CHANGE
OBSERVE AND HERE YOU'LL SEE
ON THE SAME DAY COME
SEVEN YEARS MY HUSBANDS
LAID BY ME.

In the year 1743 as Lord Duncannon was
passing through Eyam dale, he was so struck
with the beauty of a piece of fluor spar, called
in Derbyshire Blue John, which his horse
happened to tread upon, that he sent it to
Mr. H. Watson, of Bakewell, to be formed
into a vase; and hence it is, that the manu-
facturing of the various elegant articles into
which this substance has since been converted,
dates its origin.

In the month of Nov. 1755, when no fewer
than seventy thousand persons were destroyed

by an earthquake at Lisbon, the waters, of the
lakes especially, in England and Scotland
were violently agitated : at the same time loud
explosions, as of cannon, and rumbling sounds
were heard by men at work in the lead mines
at *Eyam Edge;* and no solution of these phe-
nomena could be given, till news arrived of
the dreadful catastrophe at Lisbon. On this
occasion, by an act of generosity beyond all
praise, the British Parliament immediately vo-
ted the sum of one hundred thousand pounds,
for the use of the miserable survivors; and
supplies to that amount in corn, flour, rice,
and other necessaries were shipped without
delay for Portugal, which proved a most welcome and seasonable relief.

THE WYE AND CHEE TOR.

The road from Bakewell to Buxton passes through Ashford, then by the end of Monsal Dale, and up deep vallies to Taddington; it afterwards winds along a lofty and precipitous mountain called Topley Pike, commanding a bird's eye view of the river Wye far beneath it; it then descends to the river and attends it amidst fine rock scenery, till it crosses the water by a handsome bridge lately erected at the entrance into Buxton.

The *Wye,* has its source in a hollow at the foot of Ax-edge, about one mile from Buxton. While only a small rivulet, it takes its course through a plantation, in the midst of which a pleasant walk has been formed, and afterwards runs under the Crescent: having emerged

from the village, and soon becomes a more
respectable stream, it struggles for a passage
amidst a series of ravines and deep winding
dales ; its waters meeting with frequent ob-
structions in its irregular stony channel.   One
of the most remarkable objects that oppose
its current is the rock called *Chee Tor*, distant
nearly six miles from Buxton.   This rock may
be visited by pursuing either the new or old
road to Tideswell; the former passing along
the Bakewell road, and by Soughbrook, falls
into Miller's Dale; the latter passes through
Fairfield and to a place called Hargate Wall,
four miles from Buxton, where a turn from it
to the right leads to Wormhill.   In the midst
of this village is a public house of decent
appearance called the Chee Tor Coffee House,
kept by Mr. George Hill, who conducts persons through his ground to the rock.   At
his house it is necessary to leave carriages or
horses, and proceed on foot,—first past a handsome house belonging to Sir W. C. Bagshaw,
and formerly the residence of the family of
that name; and afterwards by an irregular
descent down a steep hill, from the bottom of
which issues two extremely copious springs
making no inconsiderable addition to the river

Wye. At a sudden turn of the river near
these springs appears Chee Tor, a rock of great
magnitude indeed, but which it has long been
the custom to describe in terms of gross exag-
geration. What a late Tourist, in a fit of
spleen, has remarked concerning the Romantic Rocks at Matlock, that in " St. James's or
Hyde Park they might be attractive, perhaps
wonderful, but in Matlock Dale they really
are objects to trifling to claim attention," may
with a less degree of injustice be applied to
this Tor, which though so much celebrated, is
far exceeded by many other Derbyshire rocks
in altitude : and the great wonder is, that such
hyperbolical language, and superfinery of *picturesque* phrase, have been lavished upon it.
So it appeared to a gentleman, who lately took
his two sons to view it. Having descended
into the deep ravine, where it is situated, and
being stationed full in front of it, one of the
boys asked his father where Chee Tor was to
be found. The fact was he had previously
seen the High Tor and other rocks at Matlock,
those in Middleton Dale, and that over the
cavern at Castleton, and the view of these had
deprived Chee Tor of its marvellous features,
and caused him to look upon it without

s

any emotion of surprise. When it is said, that
" this *Giant of the Dell* lifts his ample front to
the height of near four hundred feet," if there
be any truth in the assertion, a considerable
portion of the hill above it must be included;
and if that be allowed, the calculation may be
carried to an indefinite extent: but the fact is,
that the bare rock has no such altitude, and
it is far less remarkable for its elevation
than for the great breadth of its face, which
spreads indeed along the side of the river so
as to form a sufficiently impressive object.
The scene is rendered more so by opposite
rocks, which are finely decorated with various
kinds of wood and plants, and at their farther
end approach so near the Tor, that the intermediate chasm is entirely filled by the river;
and as this, in its course, winds round the base
of the Tor, and then resumes its former direction, we may here apply the words, by which
the poet Bloomfield, surely not in a moment
of poetic inspiration, characterized another
rock, and a river of the same name;

A tower of rock, that seems to cry
Go round about me neighbour Wye.

THE PEAK FOREST.

There can be no doubt that the extensive tract of country called the *Peak Forest*, comprehending the parishes of Castleton, Hope, Chapel or Boden, and Glossop in Derbyshire, and Mottram in Longdendale, in the county of Chester, naked as it now is, was anciently covered with trees and thickets, giving shelter to wild animals, and particularly to wolves. For the extirpation of these, which were once very numerous and destructive in England, lands were granted by the crown on the condition of hunting and destroying them. This was the case at *Wormhill*, for Camden informs us, that "lands were held here by the tenure to hunt wolves," and he further observes, "now there is no danger of wolves in these places, though formerly infested by them; for the hunting and taking of which some persons held lands here at Wormhill, from whence those persons were called *Wolve-Hunt*, as is manifest from the records of the Tower."

As Wormhill has had its Wolf-hunters, so has the neighbouring small hamlet of *Tunsted* been distinguished on a quite different account, *i. e.* from its having given birth to *James Brindley*, a man whose superior judgment in planning canals, and ability in effecting them, will ever retain a principal place in the annals of inland navigation. Unfortunately he did not possess the advantages of education; and whenever difficulties occurred, it was his custom to retire to his bed, and sometimes to remain there two or three days, pondering them in his mind, and digesting schemes for surmounting them. Having completely settled his plans of operation, he was enabled by a remarkably retentive memory, without the assistance of models or drawings, to carry them into execution. It was his great reputation as an ingenious mechanic that obtained for him the patronage of the Duke of Bridgewater, on whose account he conducted a canal from Manchester to the coal works at Worsley,

He was afterwards employed in forming the
extensive canal, which he emphatically termed
the *Grand Trunk,* connecting the Trent with
the Mersey; also a branch from this uniting
it with the Severn. The system he pursued
in forming these and other canals exhibits
striking proofs of his extraordinary abilities.
It was always his object, by throwing aqueduct
bridges over rivers, by raising mounds in vallies, and by subterraneous tunnels, where necessary, to preserve, as much as possible, the
level of his canals; he was also anxious to
keep them from intefering or inosculating with
rivers in their course. In what light rivers
were regarded by him he gave a striking proof
upon his examination before a Committee of
the House of Commons, when, being asked
what he conceived rivers were created for?
his answer was, " *To feed navigable canals.*"
A kind of chronic fever, which he laboured
under some years, at length put an end to his
life at Turnhurst in Staffordshire, in 1772, and
in the fifty-sixth year of his age.

Fairfield, three miles and a half from Wormhill, and one mile from Buxton, stands on an
eminence, commanding a view of the lofty,
barren, and cheerless hills, that surround the

latter place. The church at Fairfield is a
plain, unadorned building, within which are
several monuments of persons, who having
sought in vain for a restoration to health at
Buxton, have found graves here. The following curious epitaph, if the records concerning it may be relied on, was inscribed
on a stone in the church-yard:

> Beneath this stone here lie two children dear,
> The one at Stony Middleton, the other here.

—◖◕◆▸|◀◆◕◗—

BUXTON.

Buxton is situated in an elevated part of the High Peak, and as the country around it is altogether destitute of those attractive charms which a fertile soil and a genial climate are wont to supply, its great and growing reputation can only be attributed to the efficacy of its water, the medicinal quality of which has been well known for a long course ef ages, and is universally acknowledged.

Concerning the derivation of this village's name many conjectures have been formed and advanced by different authors. To mention only two: Messrs. Lysons think it probable, that Buxton, anciently written Bawkestanes, was originally called Badestanes, from its stone baths, and that the word has been corrupted like the ancient name of Bakewell. Dr. Denman, having stated the different opinions of others, dismisses the subject with observing, that the two words, beck a brook or rivulet, and stone appear to comprise every just allusion to the name."

The temperature of the tepid water at Buxton, when it issues into the large bath, is uniformly 82°; it is very slightly impregnated with saline particles. According to Dr. Pearson's analysis, one gallon of it yielded 15¾ grains of residuum, which consisted of 1¾ gr. of muriat of soda, 2½ gr. sulphate of lime, and 11½ gr. carbonate of lime, held in solution by a slight excess of carbonic acid. From Dr. Scudamore's analysis the composition of the water appears to be, in one gallon,

Of gaseous contents.	Cubic inches.
Carbonic acid	1·50
Azote	4·64

Of solid contents.	Grains.
Muriate of magnesia	·58
—————- soda	2·40
Sulphate of lime	·60
Carbonate of lime	10·40
Extractive matter and a minute quantity of vegetable fibres }	·50
Loss	·52
	15·00

The water is used both for bathing and internally : and as a general rule, which, Dr. Scudamore says, will scarcely require any exception, it is expedient that one or two doses of suitable aperient medicines should be taken as a preliminary to the use of it. Dr. Denman, in his " Observations on Buxton Water," has given many judicious directions for its internal and external use, formed from long practice on the spot. We have his authority for saying, this water must be esteemed a very valuable medicine in certain affections of the *stomach* and *bowels*, particularly in such as arise from intemperance or debility ; and even in cases of this kind that do not properly admit of its internal use, bathing in it is often of great service.—In habitual *diarrhœas*, and in all such disorders as denote a want of tone in the intestines, this water will be found eminently useful.—In cases of *gout* attended with debility, the water may be taken with much propriety, and frequently with good effect; and though during a state of inflammation the internal use of it is carefully to be avoided, yet very few instances occur of any mischief arising from the bath under any circumstances whatever of this disorder. Frictions both in

T

and out of the bath are extremely beneficial
in the gout, and ought never to be omitted.
The different species of *rheumatism* demand
a varied method of relief; but, according to
Dr. Scudamore's remark, it is in a rheumatic
state of the constitution, unattended with
fever; when the various textures concerned
in muscular motion are so much weakened,
that the patient experiences lameness, stiffness,
and irregular pains, more particularly in damp
weather, before rain, and from a change of
wind to the east, that we see the happiest
effects of the Buxton bath.—In *scrofulous*,
and in *nephritic* disorders this water is frequently of service; also in *nervous*, and in
some *paralytic* complaints great benefit may
be derived from it: but in these cases, and
indeed in almost every other, it is advisable
to consult a physician; since great caution
in the use of so active a medicine is often
necessary. It is certain, however, that chronic
disorders alone are those, in which Buxton
water has any pretensions to celebrity: in fe-
verish and inflammatory complaints, it is found
extremely prejudicial; and in all approaches
to hectic disorders it ought religiously to be
avoided. Whenever the use of it is found to

exhaust the strength, depress the spirits, take away the appetite, excite fever, occasion or increase the action of coughing, it ought by all means to be discontinued.

The great efficacy of this water, in certain cases has been adverted to by Dr. Thomas in the following terms: "Buxton water is found of considerable service in removing many of the symptoms of defective digestion and derangement of the alimentary organs, consequent to a life of high indulgence and intemperance. A judicious use of this simple remedy, Dr. Saunders observes, will often relieve the distressing symptoms of heartburn, flatulency, and sickness; and if, persevered in, will increase the appetite, render the secretions more regular, and improve the general health and spirits, that are so intimately connected with the functions of the digestive organs. A spontanious diarrhœa is sometimes a consequence of its use at first: but it is more common, especially in habits where the action of the bowels is naturally sluggish, for a costiveness to come on during a course of this water, which must be remedied by laxative medicines."

After describing the advantages resulting

from the use of this water, Dr. Denman observes, that it cannot derogate from the reputation of Buxton, or any other medicinal water,
to assert, that the use of it is greatly assisted
by the change of air, temperance and regu-
larity in diet, avocation from business or study,
moderate exercise, early hours, and cheerful
company : and even the simple element, as it
is called, of water, though generally esteemed
the vehicle only for more powerful and more
active bodies, may itself be considered as a
medicine of great importance.—At Buxton
also a peculiar advantage is found in the
bracing quality of its air. This is generally
acknowledged, and invalids quickly become
sensible of it from receiving a remarkable
improvement of appetite, of spirits, and of
energy.—This place has, moreover, such a degree of elevation as is accounted most friendly
to animal life, which accurate observations
have determined to be from fifteen hundred to
two thousand feet above the level of the sea.

From what cause the warmth of tepid spring
water proceeds, whether from the decompo-
sition of pyrites or other mineral substances, or
from fire in the bowels of the earth, has been
the subject of many conjectures. However

this may be, the temperature of the Buxton
bath water is invariably 82° of Fahrenheit's
thermometer; and as the heat of the blood is
ninety-eight, hence it happens in bathing, that
at the instant of immersion a slight sense of
chilliness is experienced; but this in most
cases is quickly succeeded by, what may be
regarded as a sure criterion that the bath
agrees with the patient, a pleasant universal
warmth, and a general increase of elasticity.

The time usually chosen for bathing is the
morning; but **Dr. Denman** advises *invalids* to
defer it till after breakfast: the usual or prescribed exercise may be previously taken: but
the water should never be drunk immediately
before going into the bath.   The time for remaining in it may, at first, be only one or a
few minutes, and if bathing is found to agree,
it may be gradually prolonged.

There are at Buxton two public baths and
one private for gentlemen, one public and
one private for ladies, and one for the poor.
The springs have been calculated to throw up
about sixty gallons of water every minute;
and the time requisite to fill the baths is two
hours and fifty minutes.   There is also another
bath at a little distance from the village; and

the foot path through the grove or serpentine walk leads to it: the temperature of its water does not exceed 64°. A very useful accomodation of which Buxton was destitute has been supplied by the erection of hot and shower baths at the east end of the Crescent.

In cases where the internal use of the Buxton water is esteemed efficacious, Dr. Denman restricts it to a moderate quantity, and observes, that commonly two glasses, each of the size of a third part of a pint, are as much as ought to be drunk before breakfast at the distance of forty minutes from each other ; and that one or two of the same glasses between breakfast and dinner will be quite sufficient. In all cases, however, it is prudent to begin with the smallest quantity, to advert carefully to its effects, and to regulate our conduct accordingly. The water issues from fissures in a rock of blackish limestone, which forms the southern bank of the Wye, in its passage through Buxton; and it is usually drunk at an elegant building, erected by Sir Thomas Delves, and called St. Ann's Well, whither it is conveyed from the spring through a narrow gritstone channel, forty eight feet long, into a white marble basin : and this well is

regarded as one of the *seven Wonders** of
the Peak, from this circumstance, that both
hot and cold water may be obtained within
twelve inches of each other, from a double
pump, situated on the side of the building opposite to that which contains the basin.

Besides the water now mentioned, there is
betwixt the George Inn and the square, a
chalybeate spring, that issues from a shaly
stratum on the north side of the Wye, and
has a neat little dome placed over it: also, at

---

* The other reputed wonders are, Poole's Hole, the Ebbing and
Flowing Well, Elden Hole, Mam Tor, or the Shivering Mountain,
the Peak Cavern, and Chatsworth.

In the year 1678, the celebrated Thomas Hobbes, published a
Latin Poem, entitled *De Mirabilibus Pecci*, being the wonders of
the Peak, of which the following short specimen, relating to the
great efficacy of the Buxton water, may amuse some of our readers.

> Hæc resoluta senum confirmat membra trementum,
> Et refovet nervos lotrix hæc lympha gelatos.
> Huc infirma regunt baculis vestigia claudi,
> Ingrati referunt baculis vestigia spretis,
> Huc, Mater fieri cupiens, accedit inanis,
> Plenaque discedit, puto, nec veniente marito.

Thus translated, as indeed the whole of this curious poem is
said to be, by a Person of Quality,

> This cures the palsid members of the old,
> And cherishes the nerves grown stiff and cold.
> Crutches the lame unto its brink convey,
> Returning the ingrates throw them away.
> The barren hither to be fruitfull come,
> And, without help of spouse, go pregnant home.

the recommendation of Dr. Drever, the water of a spring on the Manchester road has been introduced into Buxton. Dr. Scudamore, who examined a specimen of it, says, it is remarkably pure, and free from any metallic impregnation.

There is a charitable Institution at Buxton, for the relief of such poor persons as, being properly recommended, resort to this place for the benefit of the waters. Its fund is supported by the contribution of one shilling each, paid by all visitors on their arrival, by collections at two annual sermons, and by casual donations. Every pauper invalid has the advantage of medical assistance and medicines and the use of the bath, together with an allowance of five shillings per week for the space of four weeks, if standing in need of pecuniary assistance. The Institution is under the management of a committee composed of the neighbouring gentry, and five or six hundred poor persons have sometimes been enabled by it to partake of the benefit of these salutary waters, and many of them to return to their families with renewed health and spirits, in the course of a season : and surely an institution that contributes so largely to the removal

or alleviation of human misery, can never want
the liberal support of the charitable ; and especially of those who, being restored themselves
to the blissful enjoyment of health and strength,
experience in their own persons some degree
of that transcendant happiness, which they
have the means of communicating to others.

> O! pause awhile, whoe'er thou art
>   That drink'st this healing stream;
> If e'er compassion in thy heart
>   Diffus'd its heavenly beam;
>
> Think on the wretch, whose distant lot
>   This friendly aid denies,
> Think how, in some poor lonely cot,
>   He unregarded lies.
>
> Hither the helpless stranger bring,
>   Relieve his heartfelt woe,
> And let thy bounty, like this spring,
>   In genial currents flow.
>
> So may thy years from grief and pain,
>   And pining want be free;
> And thou from heav'n that mercy gain,
>   The poor receive from thee.

Besides the benefits to be obtained from the
salutary waters at Buxton, there are others of
a very important nature, which a person may
derive from a visit to this place. If he enjoys

U

health himself, he will here become sensible
how invaluable a blessing it is, from witnessing
the severe sufferings of those who want it;
and he will be led to pity, and if it is in his
power, to assist and relieve them. If he is
young, he will learn from many lamentable
examples to what personal misery a life of dis-
sipation leads, and will be warned to abstain
from too free an use of the cup of sensual
pleasure, by the racking pains they endure who
have drained it to the dregs. If he is poor,
he will perceive from numerous instances how
unavailing riches are to secure the true enjoyment of life; he will banish that most hateful
passion, envy, from his breast, and he will
learn to acquiesce in his own humble lot.

That the warm springs at Buxton were
known to the Romans has been very generally
admitted.※   Several ancient roads met at this
place: one of them, called the Bath-way, or
Bathom-gate, commences at Brough, a Roman
station, near Hope, and was traced by the late
Dr. Pegge: another came from Manchester,
and is known in different parts of its course by
the terms High-street, Street-fields, Street-
lane, Old-gate, &c. and that which proceeded

* Dr. Denman's scepticism on this subject is remarkable.

to the south of Buxton, evident vestiges of
which appear beyond Hurdlow house, has
been already mentioned.—Specimens of Roman workmanship have also been discovered
at Buxton. Bishop Gibson mentions a Roman
wall cemented with red Roman plaster, close
by St. Anne's well, where are the ruins of the
ancient bath. This wall was taken down in
the year 1709, when Sir Thomas Delves, of
Cheshire, in memory of a cure he had received
from the waters, erected a small stone alcove
over the well; and some capacious leaden
cisterns and different articles, apparently Roman, were found in diging the foundation.
The shape and dimensions of the ancient bath,
which was about six yards from the present
bath-room, were clearly discovered, when the
building of the Crescent was commenced in
the year 1781. From these circumstances it
appears extremely probable, that the Romans
were well acquainted with Buxton, and that its
waters were anciently much esteemed. We
have no authentic information indeed on this
subject, either during their abode here, or in
the ages that succeeded their evacuation of
our island; yet the ingenious historian of
Manchester has taken the liberty of, in some

measure, supplying the defect, by thus hypo-
thetically disposing of the primeval Briton.
" The robust and hardy Briton," says he,
" whose nerves had been strung by the healthful energy of toil, now repaired to the springs
of Buxton or Bath, and stewed in the relaxing
waters. And that frivolous spirit of gallantry
and indolence, which annually crowds both
those places at present, had its commencement
at this period. He, whose blood had been
purified by a healthful simplicity of diet, now
imitated the elegance of the Roman tables.
And he, whose range was the forest and the
mountain, constructed porticos on pillars, and
affected the luxury of an airy saunter in a walk
of state."

When we descend to the times of the Reformation, we find there was then a Chapel at
Buxton dedicated to St. Ann, and through the
virtue she was believed to communicate to the
water, miraculous cures were said to be per-
formed there. It is probable that the salutary
effects experienced from the water did no little
honour to the saint; yet this did not preserve
her shrine from the exterminating zeal of the
despotic Henry, as we learn from the following
official letter addressed to lord Cromwell:

"Right Honourable my inespecial good Lord,

"According to my bounden duty, and the tenor of your lordship's letters lately to me directed, I have sent your lordship by this bearer, my brother Francis Bassett, the images of saint Ann of Buxton, and saint Andrew of Burton upon Trent, which images I did take from the places where they did stand, and brought them to my own house, within forty-eight hours after the contemplation of your said lordship's letters, in as sober a manner as my little and rude wits would serve me. And for that there should be no more idolatry and superstition there used, I did not only deface the tabernacles and places where they did stand, but also did take away crutches, shirts, and shifts, with wax offered, being things that allure and entice the ignorant to the said offering, also giving the keepers of both places orders that no more offerings should be made in those places till the king's pleasures and your lordship's be further known in their behalf.

"My Lord, I have locked up and sealed the baths and wells at Buxton, that none shall enter to wash there till your lordship's pleasure be further known. Whereof I beseech your good lordship that I may be ascertained again at your pleasures, and I shall not fail to execute your lordship's commandments to the utmost of my little wit and power. And, my lord, as touching the opinion of the people, and the fond trust they did put in those images, and the vanity of the things; this bearer can tell your lordship better at large than I can write; for he was with me at the doing of all this, and in all places, as knoweth good Jesus, whom ever have your good lordship in his blessed keeping.

"Written at Langley, with the rude and simple hand of

your assured and faithful orator, and as one ever at your commandment, next unto the king's, to the uttermost of his little power,

"WILLIAM BASSETT, Knight."

" *To Lord Cromwell.*"

In the year 1572 Dr. Jones, a physician at King's Mead, near Derby, contributed to the celebrity of the Buxton waters by a treatise on their beneficial qualities. The first convenient house for the reception of company was erected a short time previous to this publication by the earl of Shrewsbury, on the site of the building now called the Hall, a part of which belonged to the old fabric. This building occasioned the place to be much more resorted to than formerly ; but Buxton being still destitute of any other accomodation, the persons who repaired thither are said to have all slept in one long chamber together ; the upper part being allotted to the ladies, and the lower to the gentlemen, partitioned from each other only by a curtain. Mary Queen of Scots, appears to have visited Buxton four several times, while she was in the custody of the earl of Shrewsbury ; and in one of those visits that unfortunate princes applied to this place Cæsar's verses on Feltria wtih some alteration :

Buxtona, quæ calidæ celebrabere nomine lymphæ
Forte mihi posthac non adeunda, vale.

Buxton, whose fame thy milk-warm waters tell,
Whom I, perhaps no more shall see, farewell.

About the year 1670 the greater part of the old hall was taken down, and an enlarged edifice built on its site by William, third earl of Devonshire: but it is to the late duke of Devonshire that the greatly improved state of Buxton is principally to be ascribed. He either rebuilt or added to it many of its commodious inns and lodging-houses; to him it is indebted for its Crescent, Stables and new Church; he caused several walks and drives to be formed; and, by clothing different parts of the country around with plantations, he rendered its general aspect less deformed and unpleasing.

The *Crescent* is a very magnificent edifice erected from the design, and under the superintendence, of the architect Carr. The upper stories in the front are supported by an arcade, within which is a walk seven feet wide. From the top of the arches arise fluted pilasters connected at their bases by a beautiful balustrade, that skirts the whole front, the span of which is two hundred feet: a similar balustrade extends along the top of the building, and in the centre of it are the arms of the Cavendish family, neatly carved in stone, but surmounted with a pair of natural stag's horns. The number of windows in this spacious building is three hundred and seventy-eight: it is constructed of gritstone obtained near the spot, and faced with freestone procured from a quarry about a mile distant: it is now divided into one house and three hotels, called the Great, the Centre, and St. Anne's hotel. In the Great Hotel is the Ball Room, a very elegant and well proportioned apartment with a rich projecting cornice, and various appropriate and beautiful ornaments. From June to October three assemblies are usually held here every week; on Monday and on Friday an undress, and on Wednesday a dress ball. Adjoining the ball room is an elegant card room open every evening; there is also a Coffee room in this Hotel. There are several billiard tables in Buxton; an excellent one is kept by Billings opposite the hall; and on Tuesdays, Thursdays, and Saturdays, a small theatre is usually opened by a respectable company. For the diversion of gentlemen, a pack of good harriers is kept by subscription and to enjoy the amusement of shooting, many resort to the neighbouring moors, on which are found grouse, snipes, plovers, and that singular bird, the dotterell.

The hill called *Ann's Cliff*, in front of the Crescent, has been laid out by Wyatt, with all the advantage it was capable of, in beautiful slopes and agreeable promenades.

The post office is in the centre of the Crescent: it is kept by Mr. Moore, bookseller and stationer, who has an excellent public library, and a news room well supplied with papers. Another principle repository is that of Messrs. Bright under the piazza adjoining the Hall, where is a very elegant display of jewellery, cutlery, and plate, and this as well as Mr. Moore's room, is a favourite place of resort during the season.

Buxton also abounds with shops containing beautiful vases and other articles formed of the flour spar, alabaster, marble, &c. also curious specimens of minerals and fossils, similar to those exhibited for sale at Matlock and Castleton. Those quartz crystals, chiefly of the hexagonal form, called Buxton Diamonds, are found, especially after rain, on an uneven piece of ground by the Leek road, called

v

Diamond Hill, two miles and a half from Buxton: they are also found near the village of Blackwell, at a short distance from Miller's Dale and the Wye.

Near the Crescent are the *Stables*, an extensive pile, having a circular area within, sixty yards in diameter. Round this is a covered gallery, or ride, where exercise may be taken on horseback, when the weather renders shelter necessary. Near the stables is a spacious receptacle for carriages; and in completing these buildings, together with the Crescent, the Duke of Devonshire is said to have expended the sum of £120,000. His grace afterwards erected a very handsome church here, and the expense of that structure was much increased by this circumstance; the land chosen for its site was so unsound, that two thousand, two hundred piles of wood were driven into it to the depth of sixteen feet, in order to obtain a firm foundation. By an act of 51 George III, the patronage of this church or rather chapel, and that of Baslow are given to the Duke of Devonshire; and in lieu of this patronage, lands to the value of £95 per annum, and the patronage of the vicarage of Tutbury in Staffordshire, are given to the vicar of Bakewell.

The number of persons who visit Buxton during the season is so great, that some of them are occasionally obliged to seek lodgings in the neighbouring villages; though besides the different hotels already mentioned, there are several large inns, the George, the Grove, the Angel, the Eagle and Child, and the Shakespeare; which, together with the numerous private lodging houses, are computed to supply accomodation for nearly one thousand persons.

A circular road three miles in extent, passes by the *Lover's Leap*, a craggy precipice, from the summit of which a desponding lover is reported to have flung herself into the rocky gulf below. Another drive has been formed, passing in a north west direction betwixt the Macclesfield and Manchester roads, and joining the latter at the distance of three miles from Buxton. Near the Lover's Leap are many romantic masses of rock, and through an opening amidst them descends a small rill called *Shirbrook;* this is sometimes swelled by rain into a torrent, which falling over a precipice becomes a cascade of singular beauty.

When any person makes an excursion from Buxton to *Dove Dale,* he usually leaves his equipage at a farm house, called the New Inn, fifteen miles distant from Buxton, and proceeds on foot down a lane on the right that leads to the upper end of the dale.

POOLE'S HOLE.

In a vast rock of limestone at a short distance westward of Buxton, is the cavern so called, from an ancient tradition, that an outlaw named Poole once made it his residence. Its entrance is so low and contracted, that the visitor is obliged to proceed in a stooping posture nearly twenty-five yards, when the passage widens into a spacious vacuity, from the roof of which depend numerous stalactites; and to these masses and others in various parts of the cavern, from a supposed or imaginary resemblance, its mystagogues have given different names, such as the Flitch of Bacon, Poole's Saddle, his Turtle, his Wool-sack, the Lion, the Lady's Toilet, Pillion, Curtain, &c.

These imaginary objects are alluded to in the
lines of old Cotton, well known for his ludicrous
poetry.

> " Propt round with peasants on you trembling go,
> Whilst, every step you take your guides do show
> In the uneven rock the uncouth shapes
> Of Men, of Lions, Horses, Dogs, and Apes:
> But so resembling each the fancy'd shape,
> The Man might be the Horse, the Dog the Ape."

A stalagmite of surprising magnitude is
called the *Queen of Scots' Pillar*, from the
tradition of that Queen having made a visit
to this cavern, and advanced thus far into its
recesses. As this pillar cannot be passed without some difficulty, few people venture beyond
it; and indeed the remaining part of the cavern
offers few objects to repay the fatigue of ex-
ploring it. The passage contracts, and for
some yards it is necessary to descend by very
slippery and craggy steps: the passage afterwards continues on a level for eighteen or
twenty yards, when an almost perpendicular
ascent of about eighty yards commences, which
leads to a narrow fissure, called the *Eye of
St. Anthony's needle*, beyond which the steepness of the way is to be surmounted only by
clambering over irregular masses of rock.
The cavern terminates about ninety-five yards

beyond the Queen of Scots' pillar; and near
the end is an aperture through a projection of
the rock, behind which a candle is placed, when
any person has ventured to the extremity; this,
when seen from the bottom of the cavern appears like a dim star. On returning the visitor
is conducted by a way that passes underneath
a considerable portion of the road by which he
entered. The whole length of the cavern is
said to be two hundred and sixty yards.

Near Poole's Hole are numerous lime kilns
and many hundred tons of lime are burnt here
annually. The labourers and their families,
like the Troglodytes of old, reside in caves;
for no other name is so well adapted to describe habitations, which are scooped out of
the hillocks, or small mounts, formed with
the refuse from the lime kilns. The crust of
these heaps of rubbish having been conso-
lidated by time, is now impervious to the rain,
and being left of sufficient thickness, forms
a substantial roof. Each habitation contains
two or three rooms; and few have any other
light than what is admitted through the chimney and doorway. Such is the effect of the
whole, that one writer has compared them to
a rabbit warren; another observes, that, when

the workmen descend into their caves, at the
time of repast, and a stranger sees so many
small columns of smoke issuing out of the
earth, he imagines himself in the midst of a
village in Lapland.＊

＊ This accout is become less appropriate than when it was originally written, since very few, if any, are now disposed to inhume
themselves in these humble abodes.

THE MARVEL STONES.

Are situated at a short distance from Small Dale and about four miles from Buxton. They rise not more than three feet above the surface of the ground, and are found on inspection, to compose one vast rock of limestone, from sixty to eighty yards in length, and in breadth about twenty: extending longitudinally from east to west; and having its face more or less deeply indented with innumerable parallel channels or fissures, one, two, or three feet distant from each other, running in a north and south direction. The strata formed by these channels do not extend regularly throughout the rock, but are interrupted by seams or breaks which cross them, and apparently divide the whole into seperate stones of various lengths, many of

x

which have in them cavities of a round or
oblong form, that frequently contain water.
At a little distance from these lie some other
stones, that seem detached from them: but if
the intermediate soil was removed, the whole
would probably be found to belong to one
entire rock, rendered remarkable by the hori-
zontal position of its face, and the deep inter-
stices by which its strata are divided.

THE EBBING & FLOWING WELL.

The Ebbing and Flowing Well—is situated immediately beneath a steep hill, called Barmer Clough, five miles from Buxton, and by the side of the road leading to Castleton. Close to this intermitting spring is a small pool or hollow, that receives the water from several apertures by the side of it; but from these the water does not issue at regular intervals; for as that depends on the quantity of rain which has fallen, it has sometimes, though rarely, happened in very dry seasons, that the well has ceased to flow for two, three or four weeks together. Sometimes it flows only once in twelve hours; sometimes every hour; and in very wet weather, perhaps twice or thrice within that space. When it begins to rise, the motion of the water is at first gentle ; but in a short time the quantity that issues becomes very large: it continues to flow, with a gurgling noise, four minutes and a half; and it has been calculated that, in the space of one minute, twenty three hogsheads of water are discharged. Though the flowing of the well does not happen frequently in a dry season ; yet its appearance then is far more striking, the cavity that receives it having previously become dry.

The nature of this phenomenon will easily be conceived by those who understand the principle on which a syphon acts. It is to be supposed, that there is a reservoir of water in the hill above : and that a channel or duct, proceeding from the lower part of it, rises in its course to some height, but not so high as the reservoir itself, and afterwards descends to the pool at the foot of the hill. The water increasing in the reservoir at length begins to flow through this duct, and expels the air from it. As soon as this happens, the pressure of the atmosphere upon the surface of the water in the reservoir forces it through the duct, and continues to do so, till the supply being exhausted, and the air again admitted into the duct, the water immediately ceases to flow through it.*

The town of Tideswell has received its name from an intermitting well similar to that at Barmoor Clough; but the situation of it is now scarcely remembered, as it has long ceased to flow.

---

* Whoever is dissatisfied with the solution here given, though certainly the true one, with respect to the nature of an intermitting spring, may have recourse to a late *jet d'eau* of authorship, the *lymphatic* " Theory" of Mr. Henry Moore.

ELDEN HOLE.

Elden Hole—is a famous perpendicular chasm about three miles westward from Castleton. Its mouth is about thirty yards in length, and twelve broad in the widest part; and to prevent accidents a strong wall is erected round it. The credulity of travellers has often been grossly imposed upon by tales respecting its immeasurable depth. The falsehood of these reports was ascertained by the late John Lloyd Esq. F. R. S. who descended into it in the year 1770: he reached its bottom only sixty two yards from its mouth, the light from which was sufficiently strong to permit the reading of any print. The interior of the chasm he describes as consisting of two parts; one small like an oven, the other very spacious and in form like the dome of a glass-house; communicating with each other by a small arched passage. Here he found large masses of sparkling stalactite; and his whole account, given in the sixty-first Vol. of the Philosophical Transactions, has been confirmed by the assertions of several other persons, who have descended into this chasm at different periods, and all whose relations so nearly correspond, that it can hardly be supposed the depth of Elden Hole will again be made a question.

An account, too horrible to be repeated at length, is given of a benighted traveller being conducted by two atrocious villains, who undertook to be his guides, and threw him headlong into this dreadful gulf. The horror that is naturally excited by looking down into it, is depicted by Cotton in his own quaint manner.

"A formidable *Scissure* gapes so wide
Steep, black, and full of horror, that who dare
Look down into the *Chasm,* and keep his hair
From lifting off his hat, either has none,
Or for more modish curls, cashiers his own."

CASTLETON.

One road that leads from Chapel-en-le-Frith to this place, descends into Castleton dale by the *Winnets*, or *Windgates*, so called from the stream of air that always sweeps through the chasm : but this passage being extremely steep, another road, more circuitous, and adding upwards of a mile to the distance, has been lately carried by the foot of Mam Tor and the Odin Mine. The former road falls in a winding direction betwixt prodigious precipices, dark, rugged and perdendicular ; which presenting themselves at several turns, threaten opposition to all farther progress. At one of these turns to the left, a most beautiful view of the dale is suddenly presented to the eye, refreshing it after being long confined to the tedious uniformity of rude and hideous scenery, with a rich picture of beauty and fertility. As the prospect opens, *Mam Tor*, or the Shivering Mountain, is perceived at some distance on the left hand, towering above the other mountains, and having an elevation of full eight hundred feet above the level of the valley. The name, Mam Tor is an ancient British appellation; and the Shivering Mountain is a title it has received in modern times, from this circumstance, that being composed of shale and micaceous grit in alternate strata, the shale is continually decomposing under the action of the atmosphere, and falling in large quantities down the face of the precipice, the valley below, to the extent of half a mile, is overwhelmed with its ruins. The lines of an ancient encampment, which occupied its summit, are still in excellent preservation, with the exception that a number of yards are destroyed by the crumbling of the shale; the noise of which in its descent, is sometimes so loud as to be heard at Castleton, though about a mile and a half distant.

Near the bottom of Mam Tor is the very ancient mine named after the chief Saxon Deity, *Odin*. It consists of two levels running

Y

horizontally into the mountain: the upper one
a cart-gate, by which the ore is brought from
the mine; the lower a water level, to drain
the works, which have been carried more than
a mile from the entrance. It extends into the
mountain where the Blue John is found: and
the two mines, in which this valuable fluor
spar is procured, are named the Traycliff and
Waterhull. The entrance into the former is
an arched descent, conducting by numerous
steps to the depth of about sixty yards: a confined, yet tolerably easy path afterwards leads
into an opening about thirty yards deeper.
This forms the commencement of a range of
natural caverns, or fissures, in the bowels of
the mountain, the termination of which is un-
known; though, if the account that has been
given of them were worthy of credit, they
have been followed to the extent of nearly
three miles. These subterraneous passages
are extremely rude and difficult: some beautiful snow-white stalactite decorates several
parts of them; and beds of a very rich kind
of red ochre are found among the productions
of this singular mountain.

Beyond Mam Tor, when a view is taken
from the Winnets, appears a singular eminence

called *Lose Hill;* and on the summit of the
distant range of mountains beyond the dale
is seen a very remarkable knob, called *Win
Hill*; names derived, as tradition reports,
from the event of a battle fought by two con-
tending parties which had been posted at
those places.

The *Speedwell Level* or *Navigation Mine*,
has its entrance near the foot of the Winnets,
and extends into the mountainous range called
the Long Cliff. This level was originally
driven in search of lead ore by a company of
Staffordshire adventurers, with so little success
that, after an expenditure of £14,000, and
seven years' ceaseless labour, the works were
abandoned by them. The descent is beneath
an arched vault, by a flight of one hundred
and six steps, which lead to the sough, or
level, where a boat is ready for the reception of
the visitor, who is carried in it along the stream;
the guide impelling the boat by means of
wooden pegs driven into the sides of the rock.
At the distance of six hundred and fifty yards
from the entrance, the level opens with a tremendous gulph, whose roof and bottom are
totally invisible; but across which the canal
has been carried by flinging a strong arch

over a part of the fissure, where the rocks are least seperated. Here leaving the boat, and ascending a stage erected above the level, the attention of the visitor is directed to the dark recesses of the abyss beneath his feet; and firm indeed must be his resolution, if he can contemplate its depths unmoved, or hear them described without an involuntary shudder. To the depth of ninety feet all is vacuity and gloom; but beyond that commences a pool of stygian waters, not unaptly named the *Bottomless Pitt*; whose prodigious range may in some measure be conceived from the circumstance of having swallowed up more than forty thousand tons of the rubbish occasioned by blasting the rock, without any apparent diminution in its extent. The superfluous water of the level falls through a water gate into this profound caldron with the noise of a rushing torrent. This fissure is said to be nearly two hundred and eighty yards below the surface of the mountain; and so great is its reach upwards, that rockets of sufficient strength to ascend four hundred and fifty feet have been fired without rendering the roof visible. The effect of a Bengal light discharged in this most stupendous cavity is ex-

tremely magnificent and striking. Beyond
the fissure the level has been driven to a great
extent : but in this part of it little occurs that
is entitled to observation.

Upon descending into the luxuriant vale of
Castleton a very impressive effect is produced
by the contrast it forms with the bleak and elevated tracts that environ it. Its breadth in
its widest part, is two miles, and its length
between five and six : the village of Hope
situated within its limits, with its spire church,
forms a very agreeable feature, when the vale
is viewed from the descent into it. As the
road winds along the declivity, the traveller
obtains a prospect of *Castleton,* which appears
clustered near the bottom of the steep eminence at whose foot the famous cavern discloses
itself, and whose summit is occupied by the
ruins of the castle that gave name to the place.
This castle was a small structure, but a place of
great strength, being inaccessible on account
of precipices, on every side except the north ;
and even here the approach was necessarily
made by traverses to obviate the steepness of
the ascent. It appears to have originally consisted of a plain wall inclosing an area of moderate dimensions, with two small towers on

the north side, and a keep near the south-west corner, being a square tower, measuring thirty-eight feet on the outside, and twenty-one feet by nineteen within the walls; and a great part of this keep is still remaining. Mr. King, who has minutely described this fortress in the sixth volume of the Archæologia, imagines it was erected during the Saxon Heptarchy: but others suppose it was built by William Peverel, natural son of the conqueror; and its ancient appellation of *Peverel's place in the Peke,* countenances this opinion. Whatever was the fact it is certain that Peverel possessed it at the time of the domesday survey, by the name of the Castle of the Peke, with the honor and forest, and thirteen other lordships in the County of Derby. These possessions were forfeited by the grandson of William Peverel, and the Castle was granted by the crown to several persons successively: at length, in the forty-sixth year of Edward the third, it was given to his son, John of Gaunt; and from that time it has descended in the same manner as the duchy of Lancaster. The present constable of it is the Duke of Devonshire. The successors of the Peverels, to this day, hold courts of peculiar jurisdiction, in civil cases throughout the principal parts of Derbyshire and Nottinghamshire.

A tournament is reported to have been anciently held here on the following occasion. William (half brother of Pain Peverel,) Lord of Whittington, in the County of Salop, had two daughters; one of whom, named Mellet, was no less distinguished by a martial spirit than her father. This appeared from the declaration she made respecting the choice of a husband. She firmly resolved to marry none but a knight of great prowess; and her father, to confirm her purpose, and to procure a number of visitors, invited all the young men who were inclined to enter the lists, to meet at Peverels' Place in the Peke, and there decide their pretensions by the use of arms; declaring at the same time, that whoever vanquished his competitors, should receive his daughter, with his castle at Whittington. Guarine de Meez a descendant of the house of Lorrane, and an ancestor of the lords of Fitz-Warrine, hearing this report, repaired to the place above mentioned, and there engaged with a son of the king of Scotland, and with a Baron of Burgoyne, and vanquishing them both obtained the prize for which he fought.

The *Peak Cavern*, or the Devil's Cave, is one of the principal wonders of Derbyshire. It is approached by a path along the side of a rivulet, which issues from the cavern; the path leading first to a deep and gloomy recess amidst rocks that rise to a vast height on each side. On the summit towards the left, and close to the edge of the precipice, the mouldering ruins of the Peak Castle appear aloft in the air; and at the foot of the rock, on the opposite side, the cavern opens with extraordinary magnificence. Its mouth is a stupendous canopy of unpillared rock, exhibiting the appearance of a depressed arch, regular in its structure, and extending in width one hundred and twenty feet, in height forty-two, and in receding depth about ninety. Within this gulph some twine-makers have established their manufactory and residence; and the combination of their machines and rude dwellings with the sublime features of the natural scenery, has a very singular effect. Proceeding about thirty yards, the roof becomes lower, and a gentle descent conducts by a detached rock, to the interior entrance of this tremendous hollow. Here the blaze of day, which has been gradually softening wholly disappears, and the further passage must be explored by torch light. The way now becomes low and confined, and the visitor is obliged to proceed in a stooping posture, twenty or thirty yards, when a spacious opening, called the *Bell House* from its form, in the rocks, above his head, again permits him to stand upright. Beyond this the cavern seems to be entirely closed in every part; but upon a near approach to the rock, a low passage under it, almost full of water, is discovered. This opening is just large enough to admit a boat; but the passenger is obliged to lie down in it, while it is pushed to the distance of about fourteen yards under the rock, which in one part descends to within eighteen or twenty inches, from the water. Beyond the water a spacious vacuity, two hundred and twenty feet in length, two hundred feet broad, and in some parts one hundred and twenty feet high, opens in the bosom of the rock; but from the want of light, neither the distant sides, nor the roof of it can be seen. In the passage at the extremity of this vast cavern, the stream, which flows along it, spreads into what is called the *Second water :* this can generally be passed on foot, but sometimes the assistance of a guide

z

is necessary. Near the termination of this
passage is an aperture distinguished by the
name of *Roger Rain's House,* from this circumstance, that water is incessantly falling in
large drops through the crevices of the roof.
Beyond this opens another fearful hollow called the *Chancel,* where the rocks, appear much
broken and dislocated, and large masses of
stalactite incrust the sides and prominent parts
of them. Here the stranger is generally sur-
prised by a concert, which bursts from the
upper part of the chasm; and this being unexpected, and issuing from a quarter where no
object can be seen, in a place where all is still
as death, and every thing around calculated
to awaken attention, and powerfully impress
the imagination with solemn ideas, can scarcely
be heard without that mingled emotion of fear
and pleasure, astonishment and delight, which
is one of the most interesting feelings of the
mind. At the conclusion of the strain the
choristers become visible, and eight or ten
women and children, who had clambered up
by a steep ascent, appear ranged in a hollow of
the rock, about fifty feet above the station of
the spectator. From the chancel the path
leads to the *Devil's Cellar,* and thence by a

gradual descent about one hundred and fifty
feet in length, to the *Halfway House;* after
which it proceeds to a vast concavity in the
rock, resembling a bell in shape, and thence
denominated the *Great Tom of Lincoln.* The
distance from this point to the termination of
the cavern is not considerable: its whole length
is seven hundred and fifty yards, and its depth
from the surface of the mountain about two
hundred and seven. It ranges entirely in lime-
stone strata, which are full of marine exuviæ,
and occasionally exhibit an intermixture of
chert. In extremely wet weather this cavern
cannot be visited, as the water fills up a great
part of it, and rises to a considerable height,
even near the entrance: at other times the
access is not very difficult.

Bagshaw Cavern, the property of Sir **W. C.**
Bagshaw, discovered a few years ago near the
village of Bradwell, two miles south-east of
Castleton, is of very considerable extent.
The entrance into it is a descent of more than
one hundred steps: an intermitting spring is
found in it: it has no very spacious cavities;
but unlike the cavern at Castleton, it is a-
dorned with a multitude of beautiful stalactites
in the form of columns, and a profusion of

brilliant crystallizations, some of them white as snow.

In the the church at Castleton is a mural tablet, erected in memory of Mr. Micah Hall, an eminent attorney, late of that village, a person remarkable for his scepticism on religious subjects, as may be inferred from the following singular epitaph, which with the addition of his age and the time of his death, he desired to have engraven on his monument.

To the memory of
MICAH HALL, Gent.
Attorney at Law,
who died the 14th of May, 1804,
Aged 79 Years.
What I was you know not;
What I am you know not;
Whither I am gone you know not;
Go about your business.

As it was not thought proper that such an epitaph should appear in the vernacular tongue the following Latin Translation, which does no great credit to the abilities of the translator, was substituted for it.

Quid eram nescitis;
Quid sum nescitis;
Ubi abii nescitis;
Valete.